Inside the SQL Server Query Optimizer

By Benjamin Nevarez

First published by Simple Talk Publishing 2010

Editor: Chris Massey

Technical Review: Grant Fritchey

Cover Image: Andy Martin HTTP://WWW.THIS-IS-SUNDERLAND.CO.UK

Typeset & Designed: Matthew Tye & Gower Associates

Table of Contents

About the Author

Benjamin Nevarez is a database professional based in Los Angeles, California. He has more than 15 years of experience with relational databases, and has been working with SQL Server since version 6.5. Benjamin has been the technical editor of the two latest books by Kalen Delaney, including "SQL Server 2008 Internals." He holds a Master's Degree in Computer Science and has been a speaker at several technology conferences, including the PASS Community Summit.

Benjamin's blog is at HTTP://WWW.BENJAMINNEVAREZ.COM, and he can be reached at ADMIN@BENJAMINNEVAREZ.COM.

About the Technical Reviewer

Grant Fritchey, Microsoft SQL Server MVP 2009–2010, works for an industry-leading engineering and insurance company as a principal DBA. Grant has performed the development of large-scale applications in languages such as Visual Basic, C#, and Java, and has worked with SQL Server since version 6.0. He spends a lot of time involved in the SQL Server community, including speaking and blogging, and he is an active participant in the SQLServerCentral.Com forums. He is the author of several books including "SQL Server Execution Plans" (Simple Talk Publishing, 2008) and "SQL Server Query Performance Tuning Distilled" (Apress, 2008).

Acknowledgements

Writing this book was a lot of fun, but also a lot of work; actually, a lot more work than I originally expected. Fortunately, I got help from several people. First of all, I would like to thank Chris Massey. Chris helped me as the technical editor of the book, and guided me through most of the writing process, doing absolutely outstanding work. Very special thanks also go out to Grant Fritchey who helped us as the technical reviewer, and went very much beyond just reviewing, as his comments provided invaluable feedback to improve the quality of this book. Thanks also go to Tony Davis for offering me this opportunity in the first place, and helping to get the project started.

Outside the Red Gate team, my deepest gratitude goes to Cesar Galindo-Legaria, Manager of the SQL Server Query Optimization team at Microsoft, for answering my endless list of questions about the Query Optimizer, and educating me through some of the information he has published, including numerous research papers and an excellent chapter of a SQL Server book. I had the opportunity to meet Tony, Cesar, and Grant at the PASS Summit back in 2009, when I first started this journey, and I hope to finally meet Chris at the same conference in October 2011.

Although Chris, Cesar, Grant, and Tony have directly helped me to shape the content of this book, there's also a host of other people who have indirectly influenced the book through their work, which helped me to learn about, and better understand, the SQL Server query processor. With that in mind, I would like to thank the authors who have discussed the query processor in some of the available SQL Server books, Microsoft white papers and blogs, including Kalen Delaney, Ken Henderson, Lubor Kollar, Craig Freedman, Conor Cunningham and Eric Hanson.

Research papers have provided me with an unlimited source of information, and helped me to understand the Query Optimizer at a significantly deeper level than ever before. So, thanks to all that amazing work by the many people in the research community including, in addition to Cesar, Goetz Graefe, Surajit Chaudhuri, Yannis Ioannidis, Vivek Narasayya, Pat Selinger, Florian Waas, and many, many more.

Finally, on the personal side, I would like to thank my parents, Guadalupe and Humberto, and my family: my wife Rocio, and my three sons, Diego, Benjamin and David. Thanks, all, for your unconditional support and patience.

Preface

The Query Optimizer has always been one of my favorite SQL Server topics, which is why I started blogging about it, and submitting related presentations to PASS. And so it would have continued, except that, after several blog posts discussing the Query Optimizer, Red Gate invited me to write a book about it. This is that book.

I started learning about the Query Optimizer by reading the very few SQL Server books which discussed the topic, most of which covered it only very briefly. Yet I pressed on, and later, while trying to learn more about the topic, I found an extremely rich source of information in the form of the many available research papers. It was hard to fully grasp them at the beginning, as academic papers can be difficult to read and understand, but I soon got used to them, and was all the more knowledgeable for it.

Having said that, I feel that I'm in a bit of a minority, and that many people still see the Query Optimizer just as a black box where a query is submitted and an amazing execution plan is returned. It is also seen as a very complex component, and rightly so. It definitely *is* a very complex component, perhaps the most complex in database management software, but there is still a lot of great information about the Query Optimizer that SQL Server professionals can benefit from.

The Query Optimizer is the SQL Server component that tries to give you an optimal execution plan for your queries and, just as importantly, tries to find that execution plan as quickly as possible. A better understanding of what the Query Optimizer does behind the scenes can help you to improve the performance of your databases and applications, and this book explains the core concepts behind how the SQL Server Query Optimizer works. With this knowledge, you'll be able to write better queries, provide the Query Optimizer with the information it needs to produce efficient execution plans, and troubleshoot the cases when the Query Optimizer is not giving you a good plan.

With that in mind, and in case it's not obvious, the content of this book is intended for SQL Server professionals: database developers and administrators, data architects and, basically, anybody who submits more than just trivial queries to SQL Server.

Here's a quick overview of what the book covers:

- The first chapter, **Introduction to Query Optimization**, starts with an overview on how the SQL Server Query Optimizer works, and introduces the concepts that will be covered in more detail in the rest of the book. A look into some of the challenges query optimizers still face today is covered next, along with a section on how to read and understand execution plans. The chapter closes with a discussion of join ordering, traditionally one of the most complex problems in query optimization.

- The second chapter talks about the **Execution Engine**, describing it as a collection of physical operators that perform the functions of the query processor. It emphasizes how these operations, implemented by the Execution Engine, define the choices available to the Query Optimizer when building execution plans. This chapter includes sections on data access operations, the concepts of sorting and hashing, aggregations, and joins, to conclude with a brief introduction to parallelism.

- Chapter 3, **Statistics and Cost Estimation**, shows how the quality of the execution plans generated by the Query Optimizer is directly related to the accuracy of its cardinality and cost estimations. The chapter describes Statistics objects in detail, and includes some sections on how statistics are created and maintained, as well as how they are used by the Query Optimizer. We'll also take a look at how to detect cardinality estimation errors, which may cause the Query Optimizer to choose inefficient plans, together with some recommendations on how to avoid and fix these problems. Just to round off the subject, the chapter ends with an introduction to cost estimation.

- Chapter 4, **Index Selection**, shows how SQL Server can speed up your queries and dramatically improve the performance of your applications, just by using the right indexes. The chapter shows how SQL Server selects indexes, how you can provide better indexes, and how you can verify your execution plans to make sure these indexes are correctly used. We'll talk about the Database Engine Tuning Advisor and the Missing Indexes feature, which will show how the Query Optimizer itself can provide you with index tuning recommendations.

- Chapter 5, **The Optimization Process**, goes right into the internals of the Query Optimizer and introduces the steps that it performs without you ever knowing. This covers everything, from the moment a query is submitted to SQL Server, until an execution plan is generated and ready to be executed, including steps like parsing, binding, simplification, trivial plan, and full optimization. Important components which are part of the Query Optimizer architecture, such as transformation rules and the memo structure, are also introduced.

- Chapter 6, **Additional Topics**, includes a variety of subjects, starting with the basics of update operations, and how they also need to be optimized just like any other query, so that they can be performed as quickly as possible. We'll have an introduction to Data Warehousing and how SQL Server optimizes star queries, before launching into a detailed explanation of parameter sniffing, along with some recommendations on how to avoid some problems presented by this behavior. Continuing with the topic of parameters, the chapter concludes by discussing auto-parameterization and forced parameterization.

- Chapter 7 describes **hints**, and warns that, although hints are a powerful tool which allow you to take explicit control over the execution plan of a query, they need to be used with caution, and only as a last resort when no other option is available. The chapter covers the most used hints, and ends with a couple of sections on plan guides and the USE PLAN query hint.

Before we get started, please bear in mind that this book contains many undocumented SQL Server statements. These statements are provided only as a way to explore and understand the Query Optimizer and, as such, should not be used on a production environment; use them wisely. I hope you enjoy learning about this topic as much as I do.

Benjamin Nevarez

Chapter 1: Introduction to Query Optimization

The SQL Server Query Optimizer is a **cost-based optimizer**. It analyzes a number of candidate execution plans for a given query, estimates the cost of each of these plans, and selects the plan with the lowest cost of the choices considered. Indeed, given that the Query Optimizer cannot consider every possible plan for every query, it actually has to find a balance between the optimization time and the quality of the selected plan.

Therefore, it is the SQL Server component that has the biggest impact on the performance of your databases. After all, selecting the right (or wrong) execution plan could mean the difference between a query execution time of milliseconds, and one of minutes, or even hours. Naturally, a better understanding of how the Query Optimizer works can help both database administrators and developers to write better queries and to provide the Query Optimizer with the information it needs to produce efficient execution plans. This book will demonstrate how you can use your newfound knowledge of the Query Optimizer's inner workings and, in addition, it will give you the knowledge and tools to troubleshoot the cases when the Query Optimizer is not giving you a good plan.

This first chapter starts with an overview on how the SQL Server Query Optimizer works, and introduces the concepts that will be covered in more detail in the rest of the book. We'll also cover some of the background and challenges of query optimization and, since this book will make extensive use of execution plans, a section on how to read and understand them is included as well. The chapter closes with a discussion of join ordering, one of the most complex problems in query optimization, and shows how joining tables in an efficient order improves the performance of a query but, at the same time, can exponentially increase the number of execution plans that should be analyzed by the Query Optimizer.

Note

This book contains a large number of example SQL queries, all of which are based on the Adventure-Works database, although Chapter 6 additionally uses the AdventureWorksDW database. All code has been tested on both SQL Server 2008 and SQL Server 2008 R2. Note that these sample databases are not included in your SQL Server installation by default, but can be downloaded from the CodePlex website. You need to download the family of sample databases for your version, either SQL Server 2008 or SQL Server 2008 R2. During installation, you may choose to install all the databases or, at least, Adventure-Works and AdventureWorksDW.

How the Query Optimizer Works

At the core of the SQL Server Database Engine are two major components: the **storage engine** and the **query processor**, also called the relational engine. The storage engine is responsible for reading data between the disk and memory in a manner that optimizes concurrency while maintaining data integrity. The query processor, as the name suggests, accepts all queries submitted to SQL Server, devises a plan for their optimal execution, and then executes the plan and delivers the required results.

Queries are submitted to SQL Server using the SQL language (or T-SQL, the Microsoft SQL Server extension to SQL). Since SQL is a high-level declarative language, it only defines what data to get from the database, not the steps required to retrieve that data, or any of the algorithms for processing the request. Thus, for each query it receives, the first job of the query processor is to devise a plan, as quickly as possible, which describes the best possible way (or, at the very least, an efficient way) to execute said query. Its second job is to execute the query according to that plan.

Each of these tasks is delegated to a separate component within the query processor; the **Query Optimizer** devises the plan and then passes it along to the **execution engine,** which will actually execute the plan and get the results from the database.

In order to arrive at what it believes to be the best plan for executing a query, the query processor performs a number of different steps; the entire query processing process is shown in Figure 1-1.

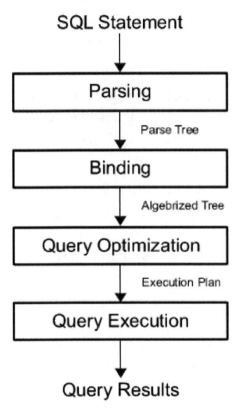

Figure 1-1: The query processing process.

We'll look at this whole process in much more detail later in the book, but I'll just run through the steps briefly now.

- **Parsing and binding** – the query is **parsed** and **bound**. Assuming the query is valid, the output of this phase is a **logical tree**, with each node in the tree representing a logical operation that the query must perform, such as reading a particular table, or performing an inner join.

- **Query optimization** – the logical tree is then used to run the query optimization process, which roughly consists of the following two steps:

  - **generation of possible execution plans** – using the logical tree, the Query Optimizer devises a number of possible ways to execute the query, i.e. a number of possible **execution plans**; an execution plan is, in essence, a set of physical operations (an Index Seek, a Nested Loops Join, and so on), that can be performed to produce the required result, as described by the logical tree

  - **cost-assessment of each plan** – while the Query Optimizer does not generate every possible execution plan, it assesses the resource and time cost of each plan it does generate; the plan that the Query Optimizer deems to have the lowest cost of those it has assessed is selected, and passed along to the execution engine.

- **Query execution, plan caching** – the query is executed by the execution engine, according to the selected plan; the plan may be stored in memory, in the plan cache.

Parsing and binding are the first operations performed when a query is submitted to a SQL Server instance. Parsing makes sure that the T-SQL query has a valid syntax, and translates the SQL query into an initial tree representation: specifically, a tree of logical operators representing the high-level steps required to execute the query in question. Initially, these logical operators will be closely related to the original syntax of the query, and will include such logical operations as "get data from the `Customer` table," "get data from the `Contact` table," "perform an inner join," and so on. Different tree representations of the query will be used throughout the optimization process, and this logical tree will receive different names until it is finally used to initialize the Memo structure, as will be discussed later.

Binding is mostly concerned with name resolution. During the binding operation, SQL Server makes sure that all the object names do exist, and associates every table and column name on the parse tree with their corresponding object in the system catalog. The output of this second process is called an algebrized tree, which is then sent to the Query Optimizer.

The next step is the optimization process, which is basically the generation of candidate execution plans and the selection of the best of these plans according to their cost. As has already been mentioned, the SQL Server Query Optimizer uses a cost-estimation model to estimate the cost of each of the candidate plans.

In essence, query optimization is the process of mapping the logical query operations expressed in the original tree representation to physical operations, which can be carried out by the execution engine. So, it's actually the functionality of the execution engine that is being implemented in the execution plans being created by the Query Optimizer, that is, the execution engine implements a certain number of different algorithms, and it is from these algorithms that the Query Optimizer must choose, when formulating its execution plans. It does this by translating the original logical operations into the physical operations that the execution engine is capable of performing, and execution plans show both the logical and physical operations. Some logical operations, such as a Sort, translate to the same physical operation, whereas other logical operations map to several possible physical operations. For example, a logical join can be mapped to a Nested Loops Join, Merge Join, or Hash Join physical operator.

Thus, the end product of the query optimization process is an execution plan: a tree consisting of a number of physical operators, which contain the algorithms to be performed by the execution engine in order to obtain the desired results from the database.

Generating candidate execution plans

As stated, the basic purpose of the Query Optimizer is to find an efficient execution plan for your query. Even for relatively simple queries, there may be a large number of different ways to access the data to produce the same end result. As such, the Query Optimizer has to select the best possible plan from what may be a very large number of candidate execution plans, and it's important that it makes a wise choice, as the time taken to return the results to the user can vary wildly, depending on which plan is selected.

The job of the Query Optimizer is to create and assess as many candidate execution plans as possible, within certain criteria, in order to arrive at the best possible plan. We define the **search space** for a given query as the set of all the possible execution plans for that query, and any possible plan in this search space returns the same results. Theoretically, in order to find the optimum execution plan for a query, a cost-based query optimizer should generate all possible execution plans that exist in that search space, and correctly estimate the cost of each plan. However, some complex queries may have thousands, or even millions, of possible execution plans and, while the SQL Server Query Optimizer can typically consider a large number of candidate execution plans, it cannot perform an exhaustive search of all the possible plans for every query. If it did, the time taken to assess all of the plans would be unacceptably long, and could start to have a major impact on the overall query execution time.

The Query Optimizer must strike a balance between optimization time and plan quality. For example, if the Query Optimizer spends one second finding a good enough plan that executes in one minute, then it doesn't make sense to try to find the perfect or most optimal plan, if this is going to take five minutes of optimization time, plus the execution time. So SQL Server does not do an exhaustive search, but instead tries to find a suitably efficient plan as quickly as possible. As the Query Optimizer is working within a time constraint, there's a chance that the plan selected may be the optimal plan but it is also likely that it may just be something close to the optimal plan.

In order to explore the search space, the Query Optimizer uses transformation rules and heuristics. The generation of candidate execution plans is performed inside the Query Optimizer using transformation rules, and the use of heuristics limits the number of choices considered, in order to keep the optimization time reasonable. Candidate plans are stored in memory during the optimization, in a component called the Memo. Transformation rules, heuristics, and the Memo will be discussed in more detail in *Chapter 5, The Optimization Process*.

Assessing the cost of each plan

Searching or enumerating candidate plans is just one part of the optimization process. The Query Optimizer still needs to estimate the cost of these plans and select the least expensive one. To estimate the cost of a plan, it estimates the cost of each physical operator in that plan, using costing formulas that consider the use of resources such as I/O, CPU, and memory. This cost estimation depends mostly on the algorithm used by the physical operator, as well as the estimated number of records that will need to be processed; this estimate of the number of records is known as the **cardinality estimation**.

To help with this cardinality estimation, SQL Server uses and maintains optimizer statistics, which contain statistical information describing the distribution of values in one or more columns of a table. Once the cost for each operator is estimated using estimations of cardinality and resource demands, the Query Optimizer will add up all of these costs to estimate the cost for the entire plan. Rather than go into more detail here, statistics and cost estimation will be covered in more detail in *Chapter 3, Statistics and Cost Estimation*.

Query execution and plan caching

Once the query is optimized, the resulting plan is used by the execution engine to retrieve the desired data. The generated execution plan may be stored in memory, in the plan cache (known as the "procedure cache" in previous versions of SQL Server) in order that it may be reused if the same query is executed again. If a valid plan is available in the plan cache, then the optimization process can be skipped and the associated cost of this step, in terms of optimization time, CPU resources, and so on, can be avoided.

However, reuse of an existing plan may not always be the best solution for a given query. Depending on the distribution of data within a table, the optimal execution plan for a given query may differ greatly, depending on the parameters provided in said query, and a behavior known as parameter sniffing may result in a suboptimal plan being chosen.

In fact, given the level of impact which query parameters can have on query performance, the parameter sniffing behavior (as well as several other parameter-related topics) will be discussed in plenty of detail in *Chapter 6, Additional Topics*.

Even when an execution plan is available in the plan cache, some metadata changes, such as the removal of an index or a constraint, or significant enough changes made to the contents of the database, may render an existing plan invalid or suboptimal, and thus cause it to be discarded from the plan cache and a new optimization to be generated. As a trivial example, removing an index will make a plan invalid if the index is used by that plan. Likewise, the creation of a new index could make a plan suboptimal, if this index could be used to create a more efficient alternative plan; and enough changes to the database contents may trigger an automatic update of statistics, with the same effect on the existing plan.

Plans may also be removed from the plan cache when SQL Server is under memory pressure or when certain statements are executed. Changing some configuration options, for example, **max degree of parallelism**, will clear the entire plan cache. Alternatively, some statements, like altering a database with certain `ALTER DATABASE` options will clear all the plans associated with that particular database.

Hinting

Most of the time, the Query Optimizer does a great job of choosing highly efficient execution plans. However, there may be cases when the selected execution plan does not perform as expected. It is vitally important to differentiate between the occasions when these cases arise because you are not providing the Query Optimizer with all the information it needs to do a good job, and the occasions when the problem arises because of a Query Optimizer limitation. As mentioned earlier, one of the purposes of this book is to give you the knowledge and tools, both to write better queries, and to troubleshoot the cases when the Query Optimizer is not giving you a good plan, and your queries are not performing well.

The reality is that query optimizers are highly complex pieces of software which, even after more than 30 years of research, still face technical challenges, some of which will be mentioned in the next section. As a result, there may be cases when, even after you've provided the Query Optimizer with all the information it needs, and there doesn't seem to be any apparent problem, you are still not getting an efficient plan; in these cases you may want to resort to hints. However, since hints let you to override the operations of the Query Optimizer, they need to be used with caution, and only as a last resort when no other option is available. Hints are instructions that you can send to the Query Optimizer to influence a particular area of an execution plan. For example, you can use hints to direct the Query Optimizer to use a particular index or a specific join algorithm. You can even ask the Query Optimizer to use a specific execution plan, provided that you specify one in XML format. Hints, and cases where you may need to use them, will be covered in *Chapter 7, Hints*.

Ongoing Query Optimizer Challenges

Query optimization is an inherently complex problem, not only in SQL Server, but in any other relational database system. Despite the fact that query optimization research dates back to the early seventies, challenges in some fundamental areas are still being addressed today. The first major impediment to a query optimizer finding an optimal plan is the fact that, for many queries, it is just not possible to explore the entire search space. An effect known as combinatorial explosion makes this exhaustive enumeration impossible, as the number of possible plans grows very rapidly depending on the number of tables joined in the query. To make the search a manageable process, heuristics are used to limit the search space (these will be touched upon again in *Chapter 5, The Optimization Process*). However, if a query optimizer is not able to explore the entire search space, there is no way to prove that you can get an absolutely optimal plan, or even that the best plan is among the candidates being considered. As a result, it is clearly extremely important that the set of plans which a query optimizer considers contains plans with low costs.

This leads us to another major technical challenge for the Query Optimizer: accurate cost and cardinality estimation. Since a cost-based optimizer selects the execution plan with the lowest cost, the quality of the plan selection is only as good as the accuracy of the optimizer's cost and cardinality estimations. Even supposing that time is not a concern, and that the query optimizer can analyze the entire search space without a problem, cardinality and cost estimation errors can still make a query optimizer select the wrong plan. Cost estimation models are inherently inexact, as they do not consider all of the hardware conditions, and must necessarily make certain assumptions about the environment. For example, the costing model assumes that every query starts with a cold cache (i.e. that its data is read from disk and not from memory) and this assumption could lead to costing estimation errors in some cases. In addition, cost estimation relies on cardinality estimation, which is also inexact and has some known limitations, especially when it comes to the estimation of the intermediate results in a plan. On top of all that, there are some operations which are not covered by the mathematical model of the cardinality estimation component, which has to resort to guess logic or heuristics to deal with these situations. Cardinality and cost estimation will be covered in more detail in *Chapter 3, Statistics and Cost Estimation*.

A historical perspective

We've seen some of the challenges query optimizers still face today, but these imperfections are not for want of time or research. One of these earliest works describing a cost-based query optimizer was *Access Path Selection in a Relational Database Management System*, published in 1979 by Pat Selinger et al., to describe the query optimizer for an experimental database management system developed in 1975 at what is now the IBM Almaden Research Center. This database management system, called "System R," advanced the field of query optimization by introducing the use of cost-based query optimization, the use of statistics, an efficient method of determining join orders, and the addition of CPU cost to the optimizer's cost estimation formulae.

Yet, despite being an enormous influence in the field of query optimization research, it suffered a major drawback: its framework could not be easily extended to include additional transformations. This led to the development of more extensible optimization architectures, which facilitated the gradual addition of new functionality to query optimizers. The trailblazers in this field were the Exodus Optimizer Generator, defined by Goetz Graefe and David DeWitt and, later, the Volcano Optimizer Generator, defined by Goetz Graefe and William McKenna. Goetz Graefe then went on to define the Cascades Framework, resolving errors which were present in his previous two endeavors.

While this is interesting, what's most relevant for you and me is that SQL Server implemented its own cost-based Query Optimizer, based on the Cascades Framework, in 1999, when its database engine was re-architected for the release of SQL Server 7.0. The extensible architecture of the Cascades Framework has made it much easier for new functionality, such as new transformation rules or physical operators, to be implemented in the Query Optimizer. We will discuss transformation rules in *Chapter 5*, *The Optimization Process*, and physical operators will be discussed in *Chapter 2*, *The Execution Engine*.

Execution Plans

Now that we've got a foundation in the Query Optimizer and how it works its magic, it's time to consider how we, as users, can interact with it. The primary way we'll interact with the Query Optimizer is through execution plans which, as I mentioned earlier, are ultimately trees consisting of a number of physical operators which, in turn, contain the algorithms to produce the required results from the database. Given that I will make extensive use of execution plans throughout the book, and because it's very useful to be familiar with them in any case, in this section I'll show you how to display and read them.

You can request either an actual or an estimated execution plan for a given query, and either of these two types can be displayed as a graphic, text, or XML plan. The only difference between these three formats is the level of detail of information displayed.

However, when an actual plan is requested, the query needs to be executed, and the plan is then displayed along with the query results. On the other hand, when an estimated plan is requested, the query is naturally not executed; the plan displayed is simply the plan that SQL Server would most probably use if the query *were* executed (bearing in mind that a recompile, which we'll discuss later, may generate a different plan at execution time). Nevertheless, using an estimated plan has several benefits, including displaying a plan for a long-running query for inspection without actually running the query, or displaying a plan for update operations without changing the database.

You can display the graphical plans in SQL Server Management Studio by clicking the **Display Estimated Execution Plan** or **Include Actual Execution Plan** buttons from the SQL Editor toolbar, which is enabled by default. Clicking on **Display Estimated Execution Plan** will show the plan immediately, without executing the query whereas, to request an actual execution plan, you need to click on **Include Actual Execution Plan** and then execute the query.

As an example, copy the following query to the Management Studio Query Editor, select the **AdventureWorks** database, click the **Include Actual Execution Plan** button, and execute the query.

```
SELECT DISTINCT(City) FROM Person.Address
```

Listing 1-1.

This displays the plan shown in Figure 1-2.

Figure 1-2:   Graphical execution plan.

Physical operators, such as the Index Scan and the Hash Aggregate physical operators, seen in Figure 1-2, are represented as icons in a graphical plan. The first icon is called the result operator; it represents the SELECT statement, and is usually the root element in the plan.

Operators implement a basic function or operation of the execution engine; for example, a logical join operation could be implemented by any of three different physical join operators: Nested Loops Join, Merge Join or Hash Join. Obviously, there are many more operators implemented in the execution engine, and all of them are documented in Books Online, if you're curious about them. The Query Optimizer builds an execution plan, choosing from these operators, which may read records from the database, like the Index Scan operator shown in the previous plan, or may read records from another operator, like the Hash Aggregate, which is reading records from the Index Scan operator.

After the operator performs some function on the records it has read, the results are output to its parent. This data flow is represented by arrows between the operators; the thickness of the arrows corresponds to the relative number of rows. You can hover the mouse pointer over an arrow to get more information about that data flow, displayed as a tooltip. For example, if you hover the mouse pointer over the arrow between the Index Scan and the Hash Aggregate operators (shown in Figure 1-2), you will get the data flow information between these operators, as shown in Figure 1-3.

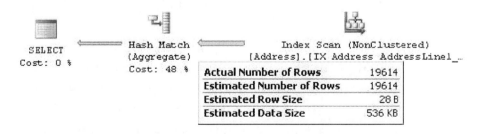

Figure 1-3: Data flow between Index Scan and Hash Aggregate operators.

By looking at the actual number of rows, you can see that the Index Scan operator is reading 19,614 rows from the database and sending them to the Hash Aggregate operator. The Hash Aggregate operator is, in turn, performing some operation on this data and sending 575 records to its parent, which you can see by placing the mouse pointer over the arrow between the Hash Aggregate and the SELECT icon.

Basically, in this instance, the Index Scan operator is reading all 19,614 rows from an index, and the Hash Aggregate is processing these rows to obtain the list of distinct cities, of which there are 575, which will be displayed in the Results window in Management Studio. Notice, also, how you can see the estimated, as well as the actual, number of rows; this is the Query Optimizer's cardinality estimation for this operator. Comparing the actual and the estimated number of rows can help you to detect cardinality estimation errors, which can affect the quality of your execution plans, as will be discussed in *Chapter 3*, *Statistics and Cost Estimation*.

To perform their job, physical operators implement at least the following three methods: **Open()**, which causes an operator to be initialized, **GetRow()** to request a row from the operator, and **Close()** to shut down the operator once it has performed its role. An operator can request rows from other operators by calling their **GetRow()** method. Since **GetRow()** produces just one row at a time, the actual number of rows displayed in the execution plan is also the number of times the method was called on a specific operator, and an additional call to **GetRow()** is used by the operator to indicate the end of the result set. In the previous example, the Hash Aggregate operator calls the **Open()** method once, **GetRow()** 19,615 times and **Close()** once on the Index Scan operator.

In addition to learning more about the data flow, you can also hover the mouse pointer over an operator to get more information about it. For example, Figure 1-4 shows information about the Index Scan operator; notice that it includes, among other things, data on estimated costing information like the estimated I/O, CPU, operator and subtree costs. You can also see the relative cost of each operator in the plan as a percentage of the overall plan, as shown in Figure 1-2. For example, the cost of the Index Scan is 52% of the cost of the entire plan.

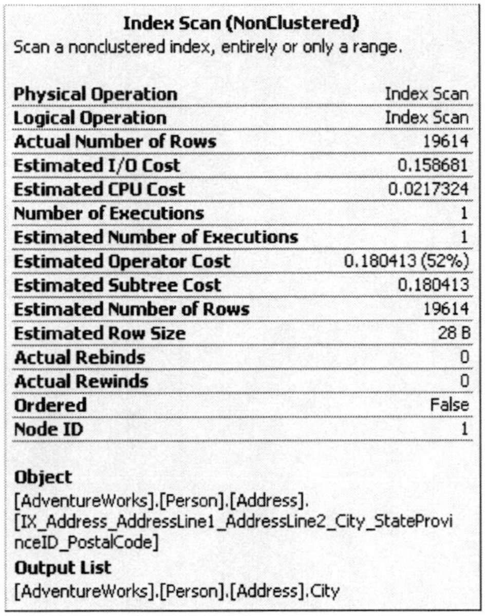

Index Scan (NonClustered)	
Scan a nonclustered index, entirely or only a range.	
Physical Operation	Index Scan
Logical Operation	Index Scan
Actual Number of Rows	19614
Estimated I/O Cost	0.158681
Estimated CPU Cost	0.0217324
Number of Executions	1
Estimated Number of Executions	1
Estimated Operator Cost	0.180413 (52%)
Estimated Subtree Cost	0.180413
Estimated Number of Rows	19614
Estimated Row Size	28 B
Actual Rebinds	0
Actual Rewinds	0
Ordered	False
Node ID	1

Object
[AdventureWorks].[Person].[Address].
[IX_Address_AddressLine1_AddressLine2_City_StateProvi
nceID_PostalCode]
Output List
[AdventureWorks].[Person].[Address].City

Figure 1-4: Tooltip for the Index Scan operator.

Additional information from an operator or the entire query can be obtained by using the Properties window. So, for example, choosing the SELECT icon and selecting the **Properties** window from the **View** menu (or pressing **F4**) will show some properties for the entire query, as shown in Figure 1-5.

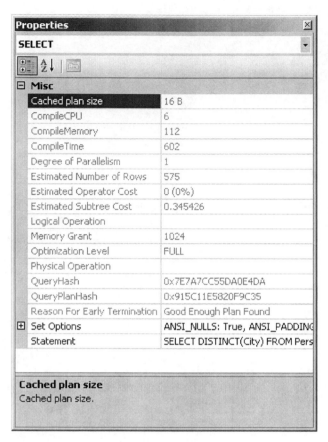

Figure 1-5: Properties window for the query.

Once you have displayed a graphical plan, you can also easily display the same plan in XML format. Simple right-click anywhere on the execution plan window to display a pop-up window, as shown in Figure 1-6, and select **Show Execution Plan XML...**; this will open the XML editor and display the XML plan as shown in Figure 1-7. As you can see, you can easily switch between a graphical and an XML plan.

Figure 1-6:   Pop-up window on the execution plan window.

```
<?xml version="1.0" encoding="utf-16"?>
<ShowPlanXML xmlns:xsi="http://www.w3.org/2001/XMLSchema-instance" xmlns:xsd=
  <BatchSequence>
    <Batch>
      <Statements>
        <StmtSimple StatementCompId="1" StatementEstRows="575" StatementId=":
          <StatementSetOptions ANSI_NULLS="true" ANSI_PADDING="true" ANSI_WAI
          <QueryPlan DegreeOfParallelism="1" MemoryGrant="1024" CachedPlanSi:
            <RelOp AvgRowSize="28" EstimateCPU="0.165013" EstimateIO="0" Est:
              <OutputList>
                <ColumnReference Database="[AdventureWorks]" Schema="[Person]
              </OutputList>
              <MemoryFractions Input="0" Output="0" />
              <RunTimeInformation>
                <RunTimeCountersPerThread Thread="0" ActualRows="575" Actuall
              </RunTimeInformation>
              <Hash>
                <DefinedValues />
                <HashKeysBuild>
```

Figure 1-7:   XML execution plan.

If needed, graphical plans can be saved to a file by selecting **Save Execution Plan As…** from the pop-up window shown in Figure 1-6. The plan, usually saved with a **.sqlplan** extension, is actually an XML document containing the XML plan, but can be read by Management Studio into a graphical plan. You can load this file again, by selecting **File > Open** in Management Studio, in order to immediately display it as a graphical plan, which will behave exactly as before.

Table 1-1 shows the different statements you can use to obtain an estimated or actual execution plan in text, graphic, or XML format. Note that, when you run any of these statements using the ON clause, it will apply to all subsequent statements until the option is manually set to OFF again.

	Estimated Execution Plan	Actual Execution Plan
Text Plan	SET SHOWPLAN_TEXT ON SET SHOWPLAN_ALL ON	SET STATISTICS PROFILE ON
Graphic Plan	Management Studio	Management Studio
XML Plan	SET SHOWPLAN_XML ON	SET STATISTICS XML ON

Table 1-1:   Statements for displaying query plans.

As you can see in Table 1-1, there are two commands to get estimated text plans; SET SHOWPLAN_TEXT and SET SHOWPLAN_ALL. Both statements show the estimated execution plan, but SET SHOWPLAN_ALL also shows some additional information, including the estimated number of rows, estimated CPU cost, estimated I/O cost, and estimated operator cost. However, recent versions of Books Online, including that of SQL Server 2008 R2, indicate that all text versions of execution plans will be deprecated in a future version of SQL Server.

To show an XML plan you can use the following commands.

```
SET SHOWPLAN_XML ON
GO
SELECT DISTINCT(City) FROM Person.Address
GO
SET SHOWPLAN_XML OFF
```

Listing 1-2.

This will display a link starting with the following text:

```
<ShowPlanXML xmlns="http://schemas.microsoft.com/sqlserver/2004 ...
```

Listing 1-3.

Clicking the link will show you a graphical plan, and you can then display the XML plan using the same procedure as explained earlier. Alternatively, you can use the following code to display a text execution plan.

```
SET SHOWPLAN_TEXT ON
GO
SELECT DISTINCT(City) FROM Person.Address
GO
SET SHOWPLAN_TEXT OFF
GO
```

Listing 1-4.

This code will actually display two results sets, the first one returning the text of the T-SQL statement. In the second result set, you will see the following plan (edited to fit the page), which shows the same Hash Aggregate and Index Scan operators displayed earlier in Figure 1-2.

```
|--Hash Match(Aggregate, HASH:([Person].[Address].[City]), RESIDUAL …
    |--Index Scan(OBJECT:([AdventureWorks].[Person].[Address]. [IX_Address …
```

Listing 1-5.

Finally, be aware that there are still other ways to display an execution plan, such as using SQL trace (for example by using SQL Server Profiler) or the **sys.dm_exec_query_plan** dynamic management function (DMF). As mentioned earlier, when a query is optimized, its execution plan may be stored in the plan cache, and the **sys.dm_exec_query_plan** DMF can display such cached plans, as well as any plan which is currently executing.

The following query in Listing 1-6 will show the execution plans for all the queries currently running in the system. The **sys.dm_exec_requests** dynamic management view (DMV), which returns information about each request currently executing, is used to obtain the **plan_handle** value, which is needed to find the execution plan using the **sys.dm_exec_query_plan** DMF. A **plan_handle** is a hash value which represents a specific execution plan, and it is guaranteed to be unique in the system.

```
SELECT query_plan FROM sys.dm_exec_requests
CROSS APPLY sys.dm_exec_query_plan(plan_handle)
WHERE session_id = 135
```

Listing 1-6.

The output will be a result set containing links similar to the one shown in Listing 1-3 and, as explained before, clicking the link will show you the graphical execution plan. For more information about the **sys.dm_exec_requests** DMV and the **sys.dm_exec_query_plan** DMF, you should go to Books Online.

If you're not yet familiar with execution plans in all their myriad forms, this section should have given you enough background to follow along through the rest of the book. We'll cover more topics and skills as we go along, but, in the meantime, let's take a look at one of the most fundamental puzzles of query optimization.

Join Orders

Join ordering is one of the most complex problems in query optimization, and one that has been the subject of extensive research since the seventies. It refers to the process of calculating the optimal join order, that is, the order in which the necessary tables are joined, when executing a query. As suggested in the ongoing challenges briefly discussed earlier, join ordering is directly related to the size of the search space, as the number of possible plans for a query grows very rapidly, depending on the number of tables joined.

A join combines records from two tables based on some common information, and the predicate which defines which columns are used to join the tables is called a join predicate. A join works with only two tables at a time, so a query requesting data from n tables must be executed as a sequence of $n - 1$ joins, but it should be noted that the first join does not have to be completed before the next join can be started. Because the order of joins is a key factor in controlling the amount of data flowing between each operator in the execution plan, it's a factor which the Query Optimizer needs to pay close attention to.

Specifically, the Query Optimizer needs to make two important decisions regarding joins:

- the selection of a join order
- the choice of a join algorithm.

In this section I'll talk about join orders but, since the implementation of join algorithms is part of the execution engine, selecting a join algorithm will be explained in *Chapter 2, The Execution Engine*. Join order is, strictly speaking, a separate concern from the algorithms provided by the execution engine, so I'll give an overview of the former here.

As mentioned, the order in which the tables are joined determines the cost and performance of a query. Although the results of the query are the same, regardless of the join order, the access cost of each different join order can vary dramatically.

As a result of the **commutative** and **associative** properties of joins, even simple queries offer many different possible join orders, and this number increases exponentially with the number of tables that need to be joined. The task of the Query Optimizer is to find the optimal sequence of joins between the tables used in the query. To clarify this challenge, let's first clarify the terminology.

The commutative property of a join between tables A and B states that:
A JOIN B is equivalent to B JOIN A.

This defines which table will be accessed first. In a Nested Loops Join, for example, the first accessed table is called the outer table and the second one the inner table. In a Hash Join, the first accessed table is the build input and the second one the probe input. As we will see in the next chapter, correctly defining which table will be the inner and outer table in a Nested Loops Join, or the build input or probe input in a Hash Join is important to get right, as it has significant performance and cost implications, and it is a choice made by the Query Optimizer.

The associative property of a join between tables A, B, and C states that:
(A JOIN B) JOIN C is equivalent to A JOIN (B JOIN C).

This defines the order in which the tables are joined. For example, (A JOIN B) JOIN C specifies that table A must be joined to table B first, and then the result must be joined to table C. A JOIN (B JOIN C) means that table B must be joined to table C first and then the result must be joined to table A. Each possible permutation may have different cost and performance results depending, for example, on the size of their temporary results. Costing of the join algorithms will also be explained in the next chapter.

By way of an example, Listing 1-7 shows a query, taken from Books Online, which joins together three tables in the AdventureWorks database. Click **Include Actual Execution Plan** and execute the query.

```
SELECT FirstName, LastName
FROM Person.Contact AS C
    JOIN Sales.Individual AS I
        ON C.ContactID = I.ContactID
    JOIN Sales.Customer AS Cu
        ON I.CustomerID = Cu.CustomerID
WHERE Cu.CustomerType = 'I'
```

Listing 1-7.

By looking at the resultant execution plan, shown on Figure 1-8, you can see that the Query Optimizer is not using the same join order as that specified in the query; it found a more efficient one instead. The join order as expressed in the query is (`Person.Contact JOIN Sales.Individual`) `JOIN Sales.Customer`. However, you will see from the plan shown in Figure 1-8 that the Query Optimizer actually chose the join order (`Sales.Customer JOIN Sales.Individual`) `JOIN Person.Contact`.

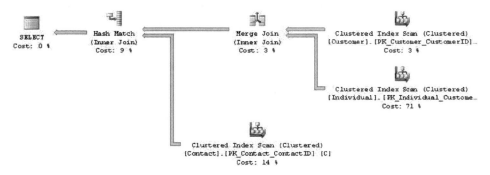

Figure 1-8:   Execution plan for query joining three tables.

You should also notice that the Query Optimizer chose a Merge Join operator to implement the join between the first two tables, then a Hash Join operator to join the result to the `Person.Contact` table.

Just to experiment, the query shown in Listing 1-8 shows the same query, but this time using the **FORCE ORDER** hint to instruct the Query Optimizer to join the tables in the exact order indicated in the query. Paste this query into the same query window in

37

Management Studio as the one from Listing 1-7, and execute both of them together, capturing their execution plans.

```
SELECT FirstName, LastName
FROM Person.Contact AS C
    JOIN Sales.Individual AS I
        ON C.ContactID = I.ContactID
    JOIN Sales.Customer AS Cu
        ON I.CustomerID = Cu.CustomerID
WHERE Cu.CustomerType = 'I'
OPTION (FORCE ORDER)
```

Listing 1-8.

The result set returned is, of course, exactly the same in each case, but the execution plan for the FORCE ORDER query (shown in Figure 1-9), indicates that the Query Optimizer followed the prescribed join order, and this time chose a Hash Match Join operator for the first join.

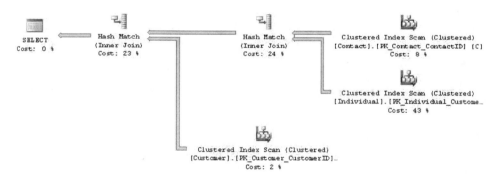

Figure 1-9:   Execution plan using the FORCE ORDER hint.

This might not seem significant, but if you compare the cost of each query, via the **Query cost (relative to the batch)** information at the top of each plan, you will see that there might be a price to pay for overruling the Query Optimizer, as it has found the hinted query to be more expensive. Specifically, the relative cost of the first query is 38%, compared to 62% for the **FORCE ORDER** query.

Estimated subtree costs

You can get the same result by hovering over the **SELECT** *icon of each plan and examining the* **Estimated Subtree Cost** *which, in this case, is the entire tree or query. The first query will show a cost of 3.2405 and the second one will show 5.3462. Therefore the relative cost of the second query is 5.3462/(3.2405 + 5.3462)*100 = 62%.*

As noted earlier, the number of possible join orders in a query increases exponentially with the number of tables. In fact, with just a handful of tables, the number of possible join orders could be numbered in the thousands or even millions, although the exact number of possible join orders depends on the overall shape of the query tree. Obviously, it is impossible for the Query Optimizer to look at all those combinations: it would take far too long. Instead, it uses heuristics, such as considering the shape of the query tree, to help it narrow down the search space.

As mentioned before, queries are represented as trees in the query processor, and the shape of the query tree, as dictated by the nature of the join ordering, is so important in query optimization that some of these trees have names, such as left-deep, right-deep and bushy trees.

Figure 1-10 shows left-deep and bushy trees for a join of four tables. For example, the left-deep tree could be: JOIN(JOIN(JOIN(A, B), C), D)

And the bushy tree could be: JOIN(JOIN(A, B), JOIN(C, D))

Left-deep trees are also called linear trees or linear processing trees, and you can see how their shapes lead to that description. Bushy trees, on the other hand, can take any arbitrary shape, and so the set of bushy trees actually includes the sets of both left-deep and right-deep trees.

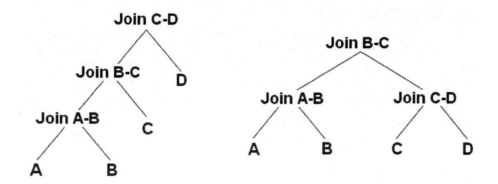

Figure 1-10: Left-deep and bushy trees.

Table 1-2 shows how the number of possible join orders increases as we increase the number of tables, for both left-deep and bushy trees, and I'll explain how it's calculated in a moment.

Tables	Left-deep trees	Bushy trees
1	1	1
2	2	2
3	6	12
4	24	120
5	120	1,680
6	720	30,240
7	5,040	665,280
8	40,320	17,297,280
9	362,880	518,918,400

Tables	Left-deep trees	Bushy trees
10	3,628,800	17,643,225,600
11	39,916,800	670,442,572,800
12	479,001,600	28,158,588,057,600

Table 1-2: Possible join orders for left-deep and bushy trees.

The number of left-deep trees is calculated as **n!**, or **n factorial**, where **n** is the number of tables in the relation. A factorial is the product of all positive integers less than or equal to **n**; so, for example, for a five-table join, the number of possible join orders is $5! = 5 \times 4 \times 3 \times 2 \times 1 = 120$.

The number of possible join orders for a bushy tree is more complicated, and can be calculated as **(2n–2)!/(n–1)!**.

The important point to remember here is that the number of possible join orders grows very quickly as the number of tables increase, as highlighted by Table 1-2. For example, in theory, if we had a six-table join, a query optimizer would potentially need to evaluate 30,240 possible join orders.

Of course, we should also bear in mind that this is just the number of permutations for the join order. On top of this, the Query Optimizer also has to evaluate a number of possible physical join operators, data access methods (e.g. Table Scan, Index Scan or Index Seek), as well as optimize other parts of the query, such as aggregations, subqueries and so on.

So how does the Query Optimizer analyze all these possible plan combinations? The answer is: it doesn't. Performing an exhaustive evaluation of all possible combinations, for a complex query, would take too long to be useful, so the Query Optimizer must find a balance between the optimization time and the quality of the resulting plan. Rather than exhaustively evaluate every single combination, the Query Optimizer tries to narrow the possibilities down to the most likely candidates, using heuristics (some of which we've already touched upon) to guide the process, which will be explained in *Chapter 5, The Optimization Process.*

Summary

This chapter has covered a lot of ground in a relatively short space, but by now you should have an understanding (or at least an appreciation) of the concepts we're going to tackle in more detail in the following chapters.

We've been introduced to the fundamental operations of the SQL Server Query Optimizer, from parsing the initial query to how the Query Optimizer tries to find the best possible execution plan for every query submitted to SQL Server. We've also looked at the complexity of the optimization process, including the challenges it faces in exploring the potentially vast search space and accurately estimating cardinality and the cost of candidate execution plans.

As a result of the research that has gone into solving some of those challenges, the Query Optimizer implemented in SQL Server is based on the extensible Cascades Framework architecture, which facilitates the addition of new functionality to the query optimizer, including new operators and transformation rules. Chapters 2 and 5 are going to go into more detail regarding both of those, and the section on how to read and understand execution plans will also have given you the basic skills to be able to find information regarding physical operators. Finally, we touched upon the problem of finding an efficient join order in a multi-join query, which is still a fundamental challenge in query optimization.

Now that we've had a first look at the concepts involved, we can start getting into the real details of how the SQL Server Query Optimizer works.

Chapter 2: The Execution Engine

The Execution Engine is, at its heart, a collection of physical operators that perform the functions of the query processor, which is to execute your query in an efficient way. Or, to look at it from the other direction, these operations implemented by the Execution Engine define the choices available to the Query Optimizer when building execution plans. The Execution Engine and its operators were briefly introduced in the previous chapter, and now we'll cover some of the most used operators, their algorithms and their costs. In this chapter, I will focus on operators related to data access, aggregations, joins, and parallelism, as these ones are the most commonly used in queries, and also the ones more used in this book. Of course, there are many more operators implemented by the Execution Engine, and you can find a complete list and description on SQL Server 2008 R2 in Books Online. Since the Query Optimizer is the primary focus of this book, this chapter will illustrate how it decides between the various choices of operators provided by the Execution Engine. For example, I will show you how the Query Optimizer reasons about choosing between a Nested Loops Join or a Hash Join, or between a Stream Aggregate and a Hash Aggregate operator.

This chapter starts with a look at the data access operations, including the operators to perform scans, seeks, and bookmark lookups on database structures like heaps and both clustered and non-clustered indexes. The concepts of sorting and hashing are also explained, showing how they impact some of the algorithms of both physical joins and aggregations, which are shown later. The next section focuses on aggregations, and explains the Stream Aggregate and Hash Aggregate operators in detail. In the same way, the joins section presents the Nested Loops Join, Merge Join and Hash Join physical operators. The chapter concludes with an introduction to parallelism and how it can help to reduce the response time of a query.

Data Access Operators

In this section, I will show you the operations that directly access the database, using either a base table or an index, examples of which include scans and seeks. A scan reads an entire structure, which could be a heap, a clustered index, or a non-clustered index. A seek, on the other hand, does not scan an entire structure but, instead, efficiently retrieves rows from an index. Therefore seeks can only be performed on a clustered or non-clustered index. Just to make the difference between these structures clear, a heap contains all of a table's columns, and its data is not stored sorted in any particular order. Conversely, in a clustered index, the data is stored logically sorted by the clustering key and, in addition to the clustering key, the clustered index also contains the remaining columns of the table. On the other hand, a non-clustered index can be defined on a clustered index or a heap, and usually contains only a subset of the columns of the table. The operations on these structures are summarized in Table 2-1 below.

Structure	Scan	Seek
Heap	Table Scan	
Clustered index	Clustered Index Scan	Clustered Index Seek
Non-clustered index	Index Scan	Index Seek

Table 2-1: Data Access operators.

Scanning

Let's start with the simplest example, by scanning a heap which, as shown in Table 2-1, is performed by the Table Scan operator. The following query on the **AdventureWorks** database will use a table scan, as shown in Figure 2-1.

```
SELECT * FROM DatabaseLog
```

Listing 2-1.

Figure 2-1:   A Table Scan operator.

Similarly, the following query will show a Clustered Index Scan operator, as shown in the plan on Figure 2-2:

```
SELECT * FROM Person.Address
```

Listing 2-2.

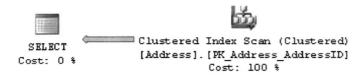

Figure 2-2:   A Clustered Index Scan operator.

Both the Table Scan and Clustered Index Scan operations are similar in that they scan the entire base table, but the former is used for heaps and the second one for clustered indexes.

Sorting is something to consider when it comes to scans, because even when the data in a clustered index is stored sorted, using a Clustered Index Scan does not guarantee that the *results* will be sorted unless this is explicitly requested. By not automatically sorting the results, the Storage Engine has the option to find the most efficient way to access this data without worrying about returning it in an ordered set. Examples of these efficient methods include an advanced scanning mechanism called "merry-go-round scanning," which allows multiple query executions to share full table scans so that each execution may join the scan at a different location. Alternatively, the Storage Engine may also use an allocation order scan, based on Index Allocation Map (IAM) pages, to scan the table. I'm not going to go into more detail regarding these techniques, because what's important right now is that they exist, and the Storage Engine has the option of implementing them.

If you want to know whether your data has been sorted, the `Ordered` property can show if the data was returned in a manner ordered by the Clustered Index Scan operator. So, for example, the clustering key of the `Person.Address` table is `AddressID`, and if you run the following query and look at the tooltip of the Clustered Index Scan operator, you will get something similar to what is shown in Figure 2-3.

```
SELECT * FROM Person.Address
ORDER BY AddressID
```

Listing 2-3.

Clustered Index Scan (Clustered)	
Scanning a clustered index, entirely or only a range.	
Physical Operation	Clustered Index Scan
Logical Operation	Clustered Index Scan
Actual Number of Rows	19614
Estimated I/O Cost	0.20831
Estimated CPU Cost	0.0217324
Estimated Number of Executions	1
Number of Executions	1
Estimated Operator Cost	0.230043 (100%)
Estimated Subtree Cost	0.230043
Estimated Number of Rows	19614
Estimated Row Size	214 B
Actual Rebinds	0
Actual Rewinds	0
Ordered	True
Node ID	0

Object
[AdventureWorks].[Person].[Address].
[PK_Address_AddressID]
Output List
[AdventureWorks].[Person].[Address].AddressID,
[AdventureWorks].[Person].[Address].AddressLine1,
[AdventureWorks].[Person].[Address].AddressLine2,
[AdventureWorks].[Person].[Address].City, [AdventureWorks].
[Person].[Address].StateProvinceID, [AdventureWorks].
[Person].[Address].PostalCode, [AdventureWorks].[Person].
[Address].rowguid, [AdventureWorks].[Person].
[Address].ModifiedDate

Figure 2-3:   Properties of the Clustered Index Scan operator.

Notice that the `Ordered` property shows `True`. If you run the same query without the `ORDER BY` clause, the `Ordered` property will, unsurprisingly, show `False`. In some other cases, SQL Server can benefit from reading the table in the order specified by the clustered index. One example is shown later in this chapter in Figure 2-15, where a Stream Aggregate operator can benefit from the fact that a Clustered Index Scan operator can easily obtain the data already sorted.

Next, I will show you an example of an Index Scan operator. This example uses a non-clustered index to cover a query; that is, it can solve the entire query without accessing the base table (bearing in mind that a non-clustered index usually contains only a few of the columns of the table). Run the following query, which will show the plan in Figure 2-4.

```
SELECT AddressID, City, StateProvinceID FROM Person.Address
```
Listing 2-4.

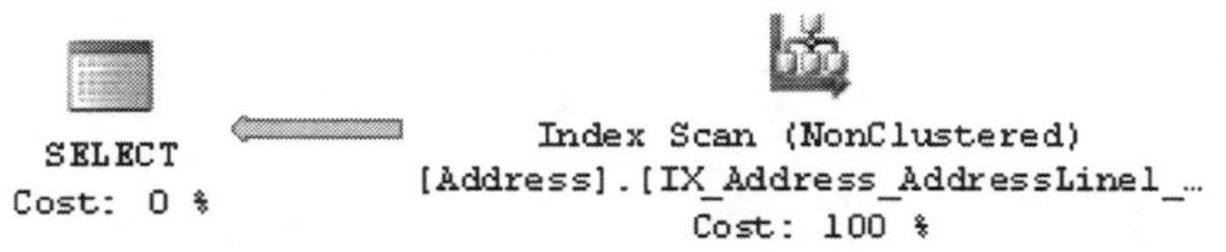

```
                                              Index Scan (NonClustered)
   SELECT                                 [Address].[IX_Address_AddressLine1_...
   Cost: 0 %                                       Cost: 100 %
```

Figure 2-4:   An Index Scan operator.

Note that the Query Optimizer was able to solve this query without even accessing the base table `Person.Address`, and instead decided to scan the `IX_Address_AddressLine1_AddressLine2_City_StateProvinceID_PostalCode` index, which comprises fewer pages. The index definition includes `AddressLine1`, `AddressLine2`, `City`, `StateProvinceID` and `PostalCode`, so it can clearly cover columns requested in the query. However, you may wonder where the index is getting the `AddressID` column from. When a non-clustered index is created on a table with a clustered index, each non-clustered index row also includes the table clustering key. This clustering key is used to find which record from the clustered index is referred to by the non-clustered index row (a similar approach for non-clustered indexes on a heap will be explained later in this section). In this case, as I mentioned earlier, `AddressID` is the clustering key of the table and it is stored in every row of the non-clustered index, which is why the index was able to cover this column in the previous query.

Seeking

Now let us look at Index Seeks, which can be performed by both the Clustered Index Seek and the Index Seek operators and which are used against clustered and non-clustered indexes, respectively. An Index Seek does not scan the entire index, but instead navigates the B-tree index structure to quickly find one or more records. The next query, together with the plan on Figure 2-5, shows an example of a Clustered Index Seek. A benefit of a Clustered Index Seek, compared to a non-clustered Index Seek, is that the former can cover any column of the table. Of course, since the records of a clustered index are logically ordered by its clustering key, a table can only have one clustered index.

```
SELECT AddressID, City, StateProvinceID FROM Person.Address
WHERE AddressID = 12037
```
Listing 2-5.

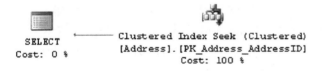

Figure 2-5:   A Clustered Index Seek operator.

The next query and Figure 2-6 both illustrate a non-clustered Index Seek operator. It is interesting to note here that the base table was not used at all and it was not even necessary to scan the entire index: there is a non-clustered index on the StateProvinceID and, as mentioned previously, it also contains the clustering key AddressID.

```
SELECT AddressID, StateProvinceID FROM Person.Address
WHERE StateProvinceID = 32
```
Listing 2-6.

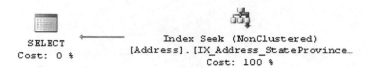

Figure 2-6:   An Index Seek operator.

Bookmark lookup

The question that now comes up is what happens if a non-clustered index is useful
to quickly find one or more records, but does not cover the query? In other words, what
happens if the non-clustered index does not contain all of the columns requested by
the query? In this case, the Query Optimizer has to decide if it is more efficient to both
use the non-clustered index to find these records quickly and also access the base table
to obtain the additional fields, or to just go straight to the base table and scan it. For
example, on the previous query on Listing 2-6, an existing non-clustered index covers
both `AddressID` and `StateProvinceID` columns. What about if we also request the
`City` and `ModifiedDate` columns on the same query? This is shown in the next query,
which returns one record and produces the plan in Figure 2-7.

```
SELECT AddressID, City, StateProvinceID, ModifiedDate
FROM Person.Address
WHERE StateProvinceID = 32
```

Listing 2-7.

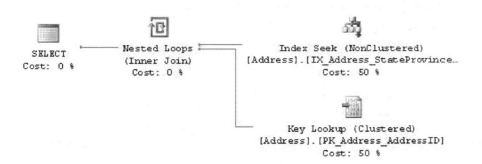

Figure 2-7: A bookmark lookup example.

As in the previous example, the Query Optimizer is choosing the index `IX_Address_StateProvinceID` to find the records quickly. However, because the index does not cover the additional columns, it also needs to use the base table (in this case the clustered index) to get that additional information. This operation is called a **bookmark lookup**, and it is performed by the Key Lookup operator, which was introduced specifically to differentiate a bookmark lookup from a regular Clustered Index Seek. Actually, the Key Lookup operator only appears on a graphical plan (and then only from SQL Server 2005 Service Pack 2 and onwards), although text and XML plans can also show if a Clustered Index Seek operator is performing a bookmark lookup. For example, run the following query:

```
SET SHOWPLAN_TEXT ON
GO
SELECT AddressID, City, StateProvinceID, ModifiedDate
FROM Person.Address
WHERE StateProvinceID = 32
GO
SET SHOWPLAN_TEXT OFF
GO
```

Listing 2-8.

The output will show the following text plan including a Clustered Index Seek operator with the **LOOKUP** keyword at the end:

```
|--Nested Loops(Inner Join, OUTER REFERENCES …)
    |--Index Seek(OBJECT:([Address].[IX_Address_StateProvinceID]),
      SEEK:([Address].[StateProvinceID]=(32)) ORDERED FORWARD)
    |--Clustered Index Seek(OBJECT:([Address].[PK_Address_AddressID]),
      SEEK:([Address].[AddressID]=[Address].[AddressID]) LOOKUP ORDERED FORWARD)
```

Listing 2-9.

The XML plan shows the same information in the following way:

```
<RelOp … PhysicalOp="Clustered Index Seek" …>
…
<IndexScan Lookup="true" …>
```

Listing 2-10.

Keep in mind that, although SQL Server 2000 implemented a bookmark lookup using a dedicated operator (called Bookmark Lookup), the operation is basically the same.

Now run the same query but, this time, request **StateProvinceID** equal to 20. This will produce the plan shown in Figure 2-8.

```
SELECT AddressID, City, StateProvinceID, ModifiedDate
FROM Person.Address
WHERE StateProvinceID = 20
```

Listing 2-11.

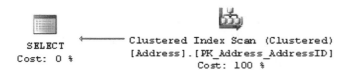

```
SELECT
Cost: 0 %
```
Clustered Index Scan (Clustered)
[Address].[PK_Address_AddressID]
Cost: 100 %

Figure 2-8: Plan switching to a Clustered Index Scan.

This time, the Query Optimizer has selected a Clustered Index Scan and returned 308 records (compared to just a single record for the StateProvinceID 32). So the Query Optimizer is producing two different execution plans for the same query, with the only difference being the value of the StateProvinceID parameter. As I will show in more detail in the next chapter, in this case, the Query Optimizer uses the value of the query's StateProvinceID parameter to estimate the cardinality of the predicate as it tries to produce an efficient plan for that parameter.

This time, the Query Optimizer estimated that more records could be returned than when StateProvinceID was equal to 32, and it decided that it was cheaper to do a Table Scan than to do many bookmark lookups. At this stage, you may be wondering at what point the Query Optimizer decides to change from one method to another. Well, since a bookmark lookup requires random I/O, which is very expensive, it would not take many records for the Query Optimizer to switch from a bookmark lookup to a Clustered Index Scan (or a Table Scan). We already know that, when the query returned one record, for StateProvinceID 32, the Query Optimizer chose a bookmark lookup. We also saw that, when we requested the records for StateProvinceID 20, which returned 308 records, it used a Clustered Index Scan. Logically, we can try requesting somewhere between 1 and 308 records to find this switch-over point, right?

Actually, as you may already suspect, this is a cost-based decision which does not depend on the actual number of records returned by query, but rather the *estimated* number of records. We (or rather, the Query Optimizer) can find these estimates by analyzing the appropriate statistics object for the IX_Address_StateProvinceID index, something that will be covered in *Chapter 3, Statistics and Cost Estimation*.

I performed this exercise and found that the highest estimated number of records to get a bookmark lookup for this particular example was 62, and the first one to have a Clustered Index Scan was 106. Let us see both examples here, by running the query with the StateProvinceID values 163 and 71. You will get the plans on Figure 2-9 and Figure 2-10, respectively.

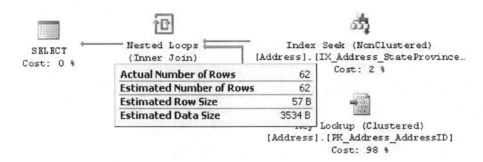

Figure 2-9:   Plan for the StateProvinceID = 163 predicate.

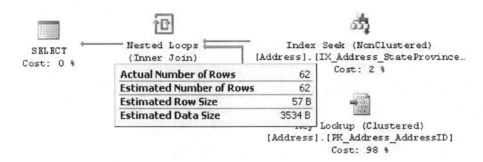

Figure 2-10:   Plan for the StateProvinceID = 71 predicate.

By looking at the plans, you can see that, for this specific example, the Query Optimizer selects a bookmark lookup for an estimated 62 records, and changes to a Clustered Index Scan when that estimated number of records goes up to 106 (there are no estimated values between 62 and 106 for this particular statistics object). Although in this case both the actual and estimated number of rows are the same, keep in mind that the Query Optimizer makes its decision based on the estimated number of rows. It does not know the actual number of rows when the execution plan is generated (as the candidate plans are only models and estimations), as the actual number of records is only known when the plan is executed and the results returned.

Finally, since non-clustered indexes can exist on both heaps and clustered indexes, we can also have a bookmark lookup on a heap. To follow the next example, create an index on the **DatabaseLog** table, which is a heap, by running the following statement:

```
CREATE INDEX IX_Object ON DatabaseLog(Object)
```
Listing 2-12.

Then run the following query, which will produce the plan in Figure 2-11:

```
SELECT * FROM DatabaseLog
WHERE Object = 'City'
```
Listing 2-13.

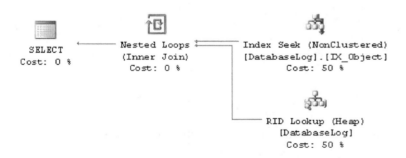

Figure 2-11:   A RID Lookup.

Note that, instead of the Key Lookup operator shown before, this plan displays a RID Lookup operator. This is because heaps do not have clustering keys like clustered indexes do, and instead they have row identifiers (RID). A RID is a row locator that includes information like the database file, page, and slot numbers to allow a specific record to be easily located. Every row in a non-clustered index created on a heap contains the RID of the corresponding heap record.

To clean up, simply remove the index you just created:

```
DROP INDEX DatabaseLog.IX_Object
```

Listing 2-14.

Aggregations

Aggregations are used in databases to summarize information about some set of data. The result can be a single value, such as the average salary for a company, or it can be a per-group value, like the average salary by department. SQL Server has two operators to implement aggregations, **Stream Aggregate** and **Hash Aggregate**, and they can be used to solve queries with aggregation functions (like SUM, AVG or MAX), the GROUP BY clause, or the DISTINCT keyword.

Sorting and hashing

Before introducing the remaining operators of this chapter, I would like to add a brief discussion on sorting and hashing, which play a very important role in some of the operators and algorithms of the Execution Engine. For example, two of the operators covered on this chapter, Stream Aggregate and Merge Join, require data to be already sorted. To provide sorted data, the Query Optimizer may employ an existing index, or it may explicitly introduce a Sort operator.

On the other hand, hashing is used by the Hash Aggregate and Hash Join operators, both of which work by building a hash table in memory. The Hash Join operator uses memory only for the smaller of its two inputs, which is defined by the Query Optimizer.

Sorting also uses memory and, similar to hashing, will also use the `tempdb` database if there is not enough available memory, which could become a performance problem. Both sorting and hashing (only during the time the build input is hashed, as explained later) are blocking or stop-and-go operations; that is, they cannot produce any rows until they have consumed all their input.

Stream Aggregate

Let us start with the Stream Aggregate operator, using a query with an aggregation function. Queries using an aggregate function and no GROUP BY clause are called **scalar aggregates**, as they return a single value, and are always implemented by the Stream Aggregate operator. To demonstrate, run the following query, which shows the plan in Figure 2-12:

```
SELECT AVG(ListPrice) FROM Production.Product
```

Listing 2-15.

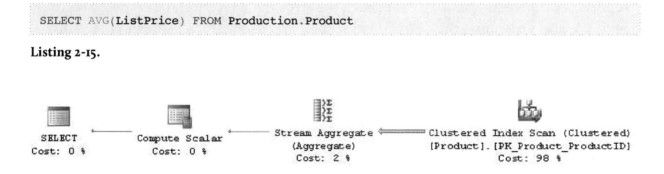

Figure 2-12: A Stream Aggregate.

A text plan can be useful to show more details about both the Stream Aggregate and the Compute Scalar operators, so you should also run the query in Listing 2-16.

```
SET SHOWPLAN_TEXT ON
GO
SELECT AVG(ListPrice) FROM Production.Product
GO
SET SHOWPLAN_TEXT OFF
GO
```

Listing 2-16.

The displayed text plan is:

```
|--Compute Scalar(DEFINE:([Expr1003]=CASE WHEN [Expr1004]=(0) THEN NULL ELSE
                       [Expr1005]/CONVERT_IMPLICIT(money,[Expr1004],0) END))
    |--Stream Aggregate(DEFINE:([Expr1004]=Count(*), [Expr1005]=SUM([Product].
                                                                [ListPrice])))
        |--Clustered Index Scan(OBJECT:([Product].[PK_Product_ProductID]))
```

The same information could be obtained from the graphical plan by selecting the **Properties** window (by pressing F4) of both the Stream Aggregate and Compute Scalar operators, and expanding the **Defined Values** property as shown in Figure 2-13.

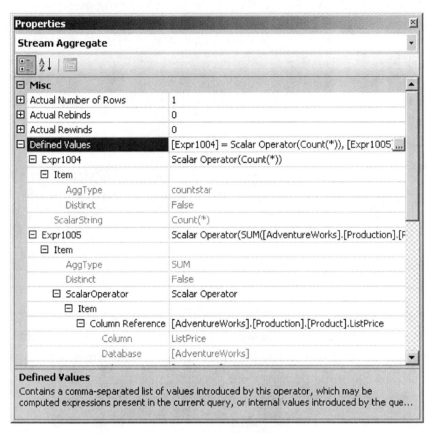

Figure 2-13: Properties of the Stream Aggregate operator.

Note that, in order to implement the AVG aggregation function, the Stream Aggregate is computing both a COUNT and a SUM aggregate, the results of which will be stored in the computed expressions Expr1004 and Expr1005 respectively. The Compute Scalar verifies that there is no division by zero by using a CASE expression. As you can see in the text plan, if Expr1004, which is the value for the count, is zero, the Compute Scalar operator returns NULL, otherwise it calculates and returns the average by dividing the sum by the count.

Now let's see an example of a query using the **GROUP BY** clause; the following query produces the plan in Figure 2-14:

```
SELECT ProductLine, COUNT(*) FROM Production.Product
GROUP BY ProductLine
```

Listing 2-17.

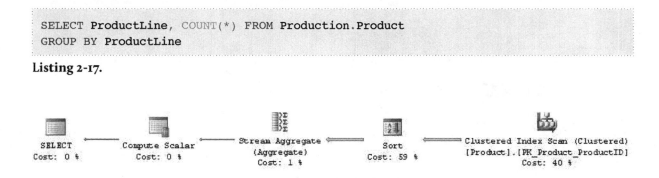

Figure 2-14: Stream Aggregate using a Sort operator.

A Stream Aggregate operator always requires its input to be sorted by the **GROUP BY** clause predicate so, in this case, the Sort operator shown in the plan will provide the data sorted by the `ProductLine` column. After receiving its input sorted, the records for the same group will be next to each other, so the Stream Aggregate operator can count the records for each group. Note that, although the first example of this section was also using a Stream Aggregate, it did not require any sorted input: a query without a **GROUP BY** clause considers its entire input a single group.

A Stream Aggregate can also use an index to have its input sorted, as in the following query, which produces the plan on Figure 2-15:

```
SELECT SalesOrderID, SUM(LineTotal)
FROM Sales.SalesOrderDetail
GROUP BY SalesOrderID
```

Listing 2-18.

Figure 2-15: Stream Aggregate using an existing index.

The Sort operator is not needed in this plan, as the Clustered Index Scan provides the data already sorted by `SalesOrderID`, which is part of the clustering key of the `SalesOrderDetail` table. As in the previous example, the Stream Aggregate operator will consume the sorted data, but this time it will calculate the sum of the `LineTotal` column for each group.

Since the purpose of the Stream Aggregate operator is to aggregate values based on groups, its algorithm relies on the fact that its input is already sorted by the **GROUP BY** clause, and thus records from the same group are next to each other. Basically, in this algorithm, the first record read will create the first group, and its aggregate value will be initialized. Any record read after that will be checked to see if it matches the current group; if it does match, then the record value will be aggregated to this group. On the other hand, if the record doesn't match the current group, a new group will be created, and its own aggregated value initialized. This process will continue until all the records are processed.

Hash Aggregate

Now let us take a look at the Hash Aggregate operator, shown as Hash Match (Aggregate) on the execution plans. This chapter describes two hash algorithms, Hash Aggregate and Hash Join, which work in a similar way and are, in fact, implemented by the same physical operator: **Hash Match**. I will cover the Hash Aggregate operator in this section, and the Hash Join operator in the next one.

The Query Optimizer can select a Hash Aggregate for big tables where the data is not sorted, there is no *need* to sort it, and its cardinality estimates only a few groups. For example, the `SalesOrderHeader` table has no index on the `ContactID` column, so the following query will use a Hash Aggregate operator, as shown in Figure 2-16.

```
SELECT ContactID, COUNT(*)
FROM Sales.SalesOrderHeader
GROUP BY ContactID
```

Listing 2-19.

Figure 2-16: A Hash Aggregate.

As mentioned earlier in this chapter, a hash operation builds a hash table in memory. The hash key used for this table is displayed on the Properties window, as the **Hash Keys Build** property, as shown in Figure 2-17, which in this case is `ContactID`. Since this table is not sorted by the required column, `ContactID`, every row scanned can belong to any group.

The algorithm for the Hash Aggregate operator is similar to the Stream Aggregate, with the exceptions that, in this case, the input data is not sorted, a hash table is created in memory, and a hash value is calculated for each row processed. For each hash value calculated, the algorithm will check if the corresponding group already exists on the hash table and, if it does not, it will create a new entry for it. In this way, the values for each record are aggregated in this entry on the hash table, and only one row for each group is stored in memory.

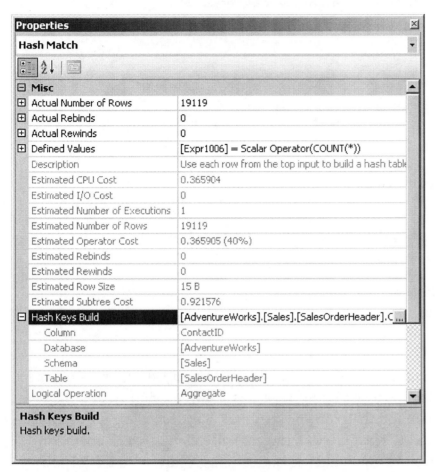

Figure 2-17: Properties of the Hash Aggregate operator, showing Hash Keys Build property.

Note, again, that a Hash Aggregate helps when the data is not sorted. If you create an index that can provide sorted data, then the Query Optimizer may select a Stream Aggregate instead. Run the following statement to create an index, and then execute the previous query again, to verify that it uses a Stream Aggregate, as shown in the plan displayed in Figure 2-18.

```
CREATE INDEX IX_ContactID ON Sales.SalesOrderHeader(ContactID)
```

Listing 2-20.

Figure 2-18: A Stream Aggregate using an index.

To clean up, drop the index using the following **DROP INDEX** statement:

```
DROP INDEX Sales.SalesOrderHeader.IX_ContactID
```

Listing 2-21.

If the input is not sorted and order is explicitly requested in a query, the Query Optimizer may introduce a Sort operator and a Stream Aggregate as shown previously, or it may decide to use a Hash Aggregate and then sort the results as in the following query, which produces the plan on Figure 2-19. The Query Optimizer will estimate which operation is less expensive: to sort the entire input and use a Stream Aggregate, or to use a Hash Aggregate and sort the aggregated results.

```
SELECT ContactID, COUNT(*)
FROM Sales.SalesOrderHeader
GROUP BY ContactID
ORDER BY ContactID
```

Listing 2-22.

Figure 2-19: A Hash Aggregate followed by a Sort operator.

Finally, a query using the **DISTINCT** keyword can be implemented by a Stream Aggregate, a Hash Aggregate or by a Distinct Sort operator. The Distinct Sort operator is used to both remove duplicates and sort its input. In fact, a query using **DISTINCT** can be rewritten as a **GROUP BY** query, and both can generate the same execution plan. If an index to provide sorted data is available, the Query Optimizer can use a Stream Aggregate operator. If no index is available, SQL Server can introduce a Distinct Sort operator or a Hash Aggregate operator. Let's see all three cases here; the following two queries return the same data and produce the same execution plan, as shown in Figure 2-20.


```
SELECT DISTINCT(Title)
FROM HumanResources.Employee
SELECT Title
FROM HumanResources.Employee
GROUP BY Title
```

Listing 2-23.

Note that the plan is using a Distinct Sort operator. This operator will sort the rows and eliminate duplicates.

Figure 2-20: A Distinct Sort operator.

If we create an index, the Query Optimizer will introduce a Stream Aggregate operator since the plan can take advantage of the fact that the data is already sorted. To test it, run this:

```
CREATE INDEX IX_Title ON HumanResources.Employee(Title)
```

Listing 2-24.

Then run the previous queries again. Both queries will now produce the plan shown on Figure 2-21.

Figure 2-21: A Stream Aggregate used by a query with a DISTINCT keyword.

Drop the index before continuing, by using this statement:

```
DROP INDEX HumanResources.Employee.IX_Title
```

Listing 2-25.

Finally, for a bigger table without an index to provide order, a Hash Aggregate may be used, as in the two following examples.

```
SELECT DISTINCT(ContactID)
FROM Sales.SalesOrderHeader
SELECT ContactID
FROM Sales.SalesOrderHeader
GROUP BY ContactID
```

Listing 2-26.

Both queries produce the same results and will use the same execution plan, as shown in Figure 2-22:

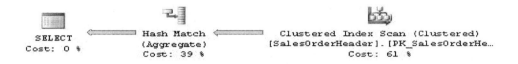

Figure 2-22: A Hash Aggregate used by a query with a DISTINCT keyword.

Joins

I started talking about joins and join orders in *Chapter 1, Introduction to Query Optimization*. In this section I will talk about the three join operators that SQL Server uses to implement logical joins: the Nested Loops Join, the Merge Join and the Hash Join. It is important to understand that no join algorithm is better than the others, and that the Query Optimizer will select the best join algorithm depending on the specific scenario, as I'll explain here.

Nested Loops Join

Let's start with a query listing employees who are also sales persons. This creates the plan in Figure 2-23, which uses a Nested Loops Join:

```
SELECT e.EmployeeID
FROM HumanResources.Employee AS e
    INNER JOIN Sales.SalesPerson AS s
    ON e.EmployeeID = s.SalesPersonID
```

Listing 2-27.

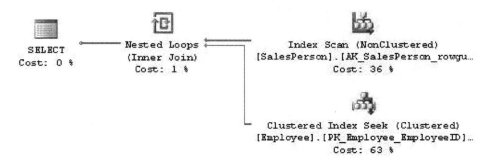

Figure 2-23: A Nested Loops Join.

The input shown at the top in a Nested Loops Join plan is known as the **outer input** and the one at the bottom is the **inner input**. The algorithm for the Nested Loops Join is very simple: the operator used to access the outer input is executed only once, and the operator used to access the inner input is executed once *for every record that qualifies on the outer input*. Note that, in this example, the plan is scanning a non-clustered index instead of the base table for the outer input. Since there is no filter on the `SalesPerson` table, all of its 17 records are returned and so, as dictated by the algorithm, the inner input (the Clustered Index Seek) is executed 17 times – once for each row from the outer table.

You can validate this information by looking at the operator properties. Figure 2-24 shows the Index Scan operator properties, where you can find the actual number of executions (which in this case is 1), and the actual number of rows (in this case, 17). Figure 2-25 shows the Clustered Index Seek operator properties, which demonstrates that both the actual number of rows and the number of executions is 17.

Index Scan (NonClustered)
Scan a nonclustered index, entirely or only a range.

Physical Operation	Index Scan
Logical Operation	Index Scan
Actual Number of Rows	17
Estimated I/O Cost	0.003125
Estimated CPU Cost	0.0001757
Number of Executions	1
Estimated Number of Executions	1
Estimated Operator Cost	0.0033007 (36%)
Estimated Subtree Cost	0.0033007
Estimated Number of Rows	17
Estimated Row Size	11 B
Actual Rebinds	0
Actual Rewinds	0
Ordered	False
Node ID	1

Object
[AdventureWorks].[Sales].[SalesPerson].
[AK_SalesPerson_rowguid] [s]
Output List
[AdventureWorks].[Sales].[SalesPerson].SalesPersonID

Figure 2-24: Properties of the Index Scan operator.

Clustered Index Seek (Clustered)	
Scanning a particular range of rows from a clustered index.	
Physical Operation	Clustered Index Seek
Logical Operation	Clustered Index Seek
Actual Number of Rows	17
Estimated I/O Cost	0.003125
Estimated CPU Cost	0.0001581
Estimated Number of Executions	17
Number of Executions	17
Estimated Operator Cost	0.0058127 (63%)
Estimated Subtree Cost	0.0058127
Estimated Number of Rows	1
Estimated Row Size	11 B
Actual Rebinds	0
Actual Rewinds	0
Ordered	True
Node ID	2

Object
[AdventureWorks].[HumanResources].[Employee].
[PK_Employee_EmployeeID] [e]
Output List
[AdventureWorks].[HumanResources].[Employee].EmployeeID
Seek Predicates
Seek Keys[1]: Prefix: [AdventureWorks].[HumanResources].
[Employee].EmployeeID = Scalar Operator([AdventureWorks].
[Sales].[SalesPerson].[SalesPersonID] as [s].[SalesPersonID])

Figure 2-25: Properties of the Clustered Index Seek operator.

Let us change the query to add a filter by TerritoryID.

```
SELECT e.EmployeeID
FROM HumanResources.Employee AS e
    INNER JOIN Sales.SalesPerson AS s
    ON e.EmployeeID = s.SalesPersonID
WHERE TerritoryID = 1
```

Listing 2-28.

This query produces the plan in Figure 2-26.

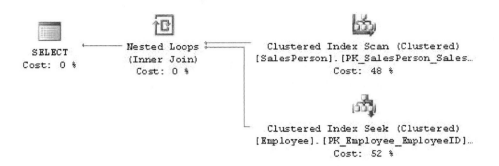

Figure 2-26: A Nested Loops Join with a filter on the outer table.

Note that the outer input is, again, `SalesPerson`, but this time it's not using an index; the new predicate is using the `TerritoryID` column which is not included in any index, and so the Query Optimizer decides to do a Clustered Index Scan instead. The filter on the `SalesPerson` table is asking for `TerritoryID` equal to 1, and only three records qualify this time. As a result, the Clustered Index Seek, which is the operator on the inner input, is executed only three times. You can verify this information by looking at the properties of each operator, as we did for the previous query.

To recap briefly, in the Nested Loops Join algorithm, the operator for the outer input will be executed once, and the operator for the inner input will be executed once for every row that qualifies on the outer input. The result of this is that the cost of this algorithm is proportional to the size of the outer input multiplied by the size of the inner input. As such, the Query Optimizer is more likely to choose a Nested Loops Join when the outer input is small and the inner input has an index on the join key. This join type can be especially effective when the inner input is potentially large, as only a few rows, indicated by the outer input, will be searched.

Merge Join

Now let's take a look at a Merge Join example; run the following query, which returns the name of each customer that is categorized as a store. The execution plan is shown in Figure 2-27.

```
SELECT Name
FROM Sales.Store AS S
    JOIN Sales.Customer AS C
        ON S.CustomerID = C.CustomerID
WHERE C.CustomerType = N'S'
```

Listing 2-29.

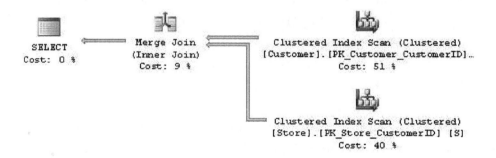

Figure 2-27: A Merge Join example.

One difference between this and a Nested Loops Join is that, in a Merge Join, both input operators are executed only once. You can verify this by looking at the properties of both operators, and you'll find that the number of executions is 1. Another difference is that a Merge Join requires an equality operator and its inputs sorted on the join predicate. In this example, the join predicate has an equality operator, is using the `CustomerID` column, and both clustered indexes are ordered by `CustomerID`, which is their clustering key.

Taking benefit from the fact that both of its inputs are sorted on the join predicate, a Merge Join simultaneously reads a row from each input and compares them. If the rows match, they are returned. If the rows do not match, the smaller value can be discarded because, since both inputs are sorted, the discarded row will not match any other row on the other input table.

This process continues until one of the tables is completed. Even if there are still rows on the other table, they will clearly not match any rows on the fully-scanned table, so there is no need to continue. Since both tables can potentially be scanned, the maximum cost of a Merge Join is the sum of both inputs.

If the inputs are not sorted, the Query Optimizer it is not likely to choose a Merge Join, although you can test this and see what the Query Optimizer does if we force a Merge Join. If you run the following query, you will notice that it uses a Nested Loops Join, as shown in Figure 2-28.

```
SELECT *
FROM HumanResources.Employee AS e
    INNER JOIN Person.Contact AS c
    ON e.ContactID = c.ContactID
```

Listing 2-30.

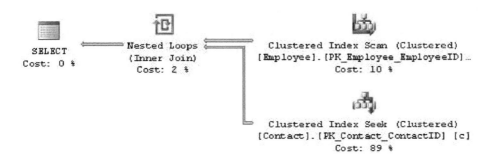

Figure 2-28: A Nested Loops Join.

73

In this case, the `Contact` table is sorted on the join predicate, but `Employee` is not. If you're curious, you can force a Merge Join using a hint, as in the following query; the Query Optimizer will introduce a Sort operator to sort `Employee` on `ContactID`, as shown in Figure 2-29.

```
SELECT *
FROM HumanResources.Employee AS e
    INNER JOIN Person.Contact AS c
    ON e.ContactID = c.ContactID
OPTION (MERGE JOIN)
```

Listing 2-31.

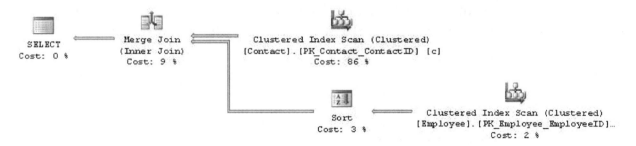

Figure 2-29: Plan with a hint to use a Merge Join.

As a summary, given the nature of the Merge Join, the Query Optimizer is more likely to choose this algorithm when faced with medium to large inputs, where there is an equality operator on the join predicate, and their inputs are sorted.

Hash Join

The third join algorithm used by SQL Server is the Hash Join. Run the following query to produce the plan displayed in Figure 2-30, and then we'll take a closer look at the Hash Join operator.

```
SELECT pv.ProductID, v.VendorID, v.Name
FROM Purchasing.ProductVendor pv JOIN Purchasing.Vendor v
    ON (pv.VendorID = v.VendorID)
WHERE StandardPrice > $10
```

Listing 2-32

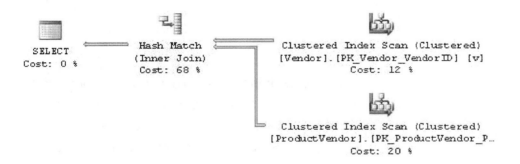

Figure 2-30: A Hash Join example.

In the same way as the Merge Join, the Hash Join requires an equality operator on the join predicate but, unlike the Merge Join, it does not require its inputs to be sorted. In addition, its operations in both inputs are executed only once, which you can verify by looking at the operator properties as shown before. However, a Hash Join works by creating a hash table in memory. The Query Optimizer will use a cardinality estimation to detect the smaller of the two inputs, called the build input, and will use it to build a hash table in memory. If there is not enough memory to host the hash table, SQL Server can use disk space, creating a workfile in `tempdb`. A Hash Join will also block, but only during the time the build input is hashed. After the build input is hashed, the second table, called the probe input, will be read and compared to the hash table. If rows are matched they will be returned. On the execution plan, the table at the top will be used as the build input, and the table at the bottom as the probe input.

Finally, note that a behavior called "role reversal" may appear. If the Query Optimizer is not able to correctly estimate which of the two inputs is smaller, the build and probe roles may be reversed at execution time, and this will not be shown on the execution plan.

In summary, the Query Optimizer can choose a Hash Join for large inputs where there is an equality operator on the join predicate. Since both tables are scanned, the cost of a Hash Join is the sum of both inputs.

Parallelism

I will finish this discussion of the Execution Engine operations with a quick introduction to parallelism. SQL Server can introduce parallelism to help some expensive queries to execute faster by using several processors simultaneously. However, even when a query may get better performance by using parallel plans, it may still use more resources than a similar serial plan.

In order for the Query Optimizer to consider parallel plans, the SQL Server installation must have access to at least two processors or cores, or a hyper-threaded configuration. In addition, both the **affinity mask** and the **max degree of parallelism** advanced configuration options must *allow* the use of at least two processors.

The affinity mask configuration option specifies which processors are eligible to run SQL Server threads, and the default value of 0 means that all the processors can be used. The max degree of parallelism configuration option is used to limit the number of processors that can be used in parallel plans, and its default value of 0 similarly allows all available processors to be used. As you can see if you have the proper hardware, SQL Server allows parallel plans by default, with no additional configuration.

Parallelism will be considered when the estimated cost of a serial plan is higher than the value defined in the cost threshold for the parallelism configuration parameter. However, this doesn't guarantee that parallelism will actually be employed in the final execution plan, as the final decision to parallelize a query (or not) will be based on cost reasons. That is, there is no guarantee that the best parallel plan found will have a lower cost than the best serial plan, so the serial plan may still end up being the better plan. Parallelism is implemented by the parallelism physical operator, also known as the exchange operator, which implements the **Distribute Streams**, **Gather Streams**, and **Repartition Streams** logical operations.

The following query, which lists the names and cities of all the individual customers ordered by CustomerID, will produce a parallel plan. Since this plan is too big to print in this book, only a section is displayed in Figure 2-31.

```
SELECT I.CustomerID, C.FirstName, C.LastName, A.City
FROM Person.Contact AS C
    JOIN Sales.Individual AS I
        ON C.ContactID = I.ContactID
    JOIN Sales.CustomerAddress AS CA
        ON CA.CustomerID = I.CustomerID
    JOIN Person.Address AS A
        ON A.AddressID = CA.AddressID
ORDER BY I.CustomerID
```

Listing 2-33.

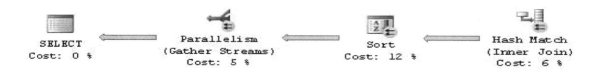

Figure 2-31: Part of a parallel plan.

One benefit of the graphical plans, compared to text and XML plans, is that you can easily see which operators are being executed in parallel by looking at the parallelism symbol (a small yellow circle with arrows) included in the operator icon. In this case, it's shown in Figure 2-31 for the Sort and Hash Join operators.

To see why a parallel plan was considered and selected, you can look at the cost of the serial plan. One way to do this is by using the MAXDOP hint to force a serial plan, as in the following query:

```
SELECT I.CustomerID, C.FirstName, C.LastName, A.City
FROM Person.Contact AS C
    JOIN Sales.Individual AS I
        ON C.ContactID = I.ContactID
    JOIN Sales.CustomerAddress AS CA
        ON CA.CustomerID = I.CustomerID
    JOIN Person.Address AS A
        ON A.AddressID = CA.AddressID
ORDER BY I.CustomerID
OPTION (MAXDOP 1)
```

Listing 2-34.

The forced serial plan has a cost of 5.31282 and, given that the default cost threshold for parallelism configuration option is 5, this clearly crosses that threshold. An interesting test you can perform in your own test environment is to change the cost threshold for parallelism option to 6 by running the following statements:

```
sp_configure 'cost threshold for parallelism', 6
GO
RECONFIGURE
GO
```

Listing 2-35.

And if you run the same query again, this time without the MAXDOP hint, you will get a serial plan with the cost of 5.31282. Since the cost threshold for parallelism is now 6, the Query Optimizer did not even try to find a parallel plan. Do not forget to change the cost threshold for parallelism configuration option back to the default value of 5 by running the following statement:

```
sp_configure 'cost threshold for parallelism', 5
GO
RECONFIGURE
GO
```

Listing 2-36.

Summary

This chapter described the Execution Engine as a collection of physical operators, which also defines the choices that are available for the Query Optimizer to build execution plans with. Some of most commonly used operators of the Execution Engine were introduced, including their algorithms, relative costs, and the scenarios when the Query Optimizer is more likely to choose them. In particular, we've looked at operators for data access, aggregations, joins and parallelism operations.

The concepts of sorting and hashing were also introduced as a mechanism used by the Execution Engine to match and process data. Data access operations included the scan of tables and indexes, index seeks and bookmark lookup operations. Aggregation algorithms like Stream Aggregate and Hash Aggregate were discussed, along with join algorithms like the Nested Loops Join, Merge Join and Hash Join. An introduction to parallelism was also presented.

Understanding how these operators function, as well as what they are likely to cost, will give you a much stronger sense of what's actually happening under the hood when you investigate how your queries are being implemented. This, in turn, will help you to find potential problems in your execution plans, and to know when to resort to any of the techniques which I'll describe later in the book.

Chapter 3: Statistics and Cost Estimation

The SQL Server Query Optimizer is a cost-based optimizer, and therefore the quality of the execution plans it generates is directly related to the accuracy of its cost estimations. In the same way, the estimated cost of a plan is based on the algorithms or operators used, and their cardinality estimations. So, to correctly estimate the cost of an execution plan, the Query Optimizer needs to estimate, as precisely as possible, the number of records returned by a given query.

During query optimization, SQL Server explores many candidate plans, estimates their relative costs and selects the most efficient one. As such, incorrect cardinality and cost estimation may cause the Query Optimizer to choose inefficient plans which can have a negative impact on the performance of your database.

In this chapter, I'll discuss the statistics used by the Query Optimizer. Statistics contain three major pieces of information: the histogram, the density information, and the string statistics, all of which help with different parts of the cardinality estimation process. I will show you how statistics are created and maintained, and how they are used by the Query Optimizer. I will also provide you with information on how to detect cardinality estimation errors that can negatively impact the quality of your execution plans, as well as recommendations on how to fix them. The chapter ends with an overview of the costing module, which estimates the I/O and CPU cost for each operator, to finally obtain the total cost of the plan.

Statistics

SQL Server creates and maintains statistics to help the Query Optimizer with **cardinality estimation**. A cardinality estimate is the estimated number of records that will be returned by filtering, JOIN predicates or GROUP BY operations. **Selectivity** is a concept similar to cardinality estimation, which can be described as the percentage of rows from an input that satisfy a predicate. A highly selective predicate returns a small number of rows. Rather than say any more on the subject here, we'll dive into more detail about these concepts later in this chapter.

Creating and updating statistics

To get started, let's take a look at the various ways statistics can be created and updated. Statistics are created in several ways: automatically by the Query Optimizer (if the default option to automatically create statistics, AUTO_CREATE_STATISTICS, is on); when an index is created; or when they are explicitly created, for example, by using the CREATE STATISTICS statement. Statistics can be created on one or more columns, and both the index and explicit creation methods support single- and multi-column statistics. However, the statistics which are automatically generated by the Query Optimizer are always single-column statistics. As I've already mentioned briefly, the most important components of statistics objects are the histogram, the density information, and the string statistics. Both histograms and string statistics are created only for the first column of a statistics object, the latter only if the column is of a string data type. **Density** information (which I'll discuss in plenty of detail later in this chapter) is calculated for each set of columns forming a prefix in the statistics object. **Filtered statistics**, on the other hand, are not created automatically by the Query Optimizer, but only when a filtered index is created, or by issuing a CREATE STATISTICS statement with a WHERE clause. Both filtered indexes and statistics are a new feature introduced in SQL Server 2008, which we will touch upon later.

With the default configuration (if AUTO_UPDATE_STATISTICS is on), the Query Optimizer automatically updates statistics when they are out of date. As noted, the Query Optimizer does not automatically create multi-column or filtered statistics, but once they are created, by using any of the methods described earlier, they *can* be automatically updated. Alternatively, index rebuild operations and statements like UPDATE STATISTICS can also be used to update statistics. Both the auto-create and auto-update default choices will give you good quality statistics most of the time, and you naturally have the choice to change this configuration, or use some other statements, if you need more control over the quality of the statistics.

So, statistics may be automatically created (if non-existent) and updated (if out of date) as necessary during query optimization. If an execution plan for a specific query already exists in the plan cache and the statistics used by the plan are out of date, then the plan is discarded, the statistics are updated, and a new plan is created. In a similar way, updating statistics, either manually or automatically, invalidates any existing execution plan that used those statistics, and will cause a new optimization the next time the query is executed.

When it comes to determining the quality of your statistics, a fact to consider is the size of the sample used to calculate said statistics. The Query Optimizer always uses a sample of the target table when it creates or updates statistics, and the minimum sample size is 8 MB, or the size of the table if it's smaller than 8 MB. The sample size will increase for bigger tables, but it may still only be a small percentage of the table.

If needed, you can explicitly request a bigger sample or scan the entire table to have better quality statistics. Using the CREATE STATISTICS and UPDATE STATISTICS statements you can specify a sample size or use the WITH FULLSCAN option to scan the entire table. Doing either of these can be of benefit, especially with data that is not randomly distributed throughout the table. Scanning the entire table will naturally give you the most accurate statistics possible. In fact, given that statistics are always created alongside a new index, and given that this operation scans the entire table anyway, index statistics are initially created with the equivalent of the WITH FULLSCAN option.

However, if the Query Optimizer needs to automatically update these index statistics, it can only use a default sample, as it may take too long to scan the entire table again.

By default, SQL Server needs to wait for the update statistics operation to complete before optimizing and executing the query; that is, statistics are updated synchronously. A new database configuration option introduced with SQL Server 2005, `AUTO_UPDATE_STATISTICS_ASYNC`, can be used to change this default and let the statistics be updated asynchronously. As you might have guessed, with asynchronous statistics update, the Query Optimizer does not wait for the update statistics operation to complete, and instead just uses the current statistics for the optimization process. This can help in situations where applications experience timeouts caused by delays related to the automatic update of statistics. Although the current optimization will use the out-of-date statistics, they will be updated in the background and will be used by any later query optimizations.

SQL Server defines when statistics are out of date by using column modification counters or **colmodctrs**, which count the number of table modifications, and which are kept for each table column. Basically, for tables bigger than 500 rows, a statistics object is considered out of date if the `colmodctr` value of the leading column has changed by more than 500 plus 20% of the number of rows in the table. The same formula is used by filtered statistics but, since they are built only from a subset of the records of the table, the `colmodctr` value is first adjusted depending on the selectivity of the filter. `Colmodctrs` are usually not exposed by any SQL Server metadata although they can be accessed by using a dedicated administrator connection and looking at the `rcmodified` column of the `sys.sysrscols` base system table in SQL Server 2008 (same information can be found on the `sysrowset columns` for SQL Server 2005).

The density information on multi-column statistics might improve the quality of execution plans in the case of correlated columns or statistical correlations between columns. As mentioned previously, density information is kept for all the columns in a statistics object, in the order that they appear in the statistics definition. By default, SQL Server assumes columns are independent so, if a relationship or dependency exists between columns, multi-column statistics can help with cardinality estimation problems in queries which are using these columns. Density information will also help on filters and **GROUP BY** operations, as we'll see in the density section later on. Filtered statistics, which are also explained later in this chapter, can also be used for cardinality estimation problems with correlated columns.

Inspecting statistics objects

Let us see an example of a statistics object and inspect the data it stores. Existing statistics for a specific object can be displayed using the **sys.stats** catalog view, as used in the following query:

```
SELECT * FROM sys.stats
WHERE object_id = object_id('Sales.SalesOrderDetail')
```

Listing 3-1.

An output similar to that in Listing 3-2 (edited to fit the page) will be shown.

```
object_id name                                                  stats_id
--------- ----------------------------------------------------- --------
642101328 PK_SalesOrderDetail_SalesOrderID_SalesOrderDetailID 1
642101328 AK_SalesOrderDetail_rowguid                           2
642101328 IX_SalesOrderDetail_ProductID                         3
```

Listing 3-2.

One record for each statistics object is shown. You can use the **DBCC SHOW_STATISTICS** statement to display the details of a statistics object by specifying the column name or the name of the statistics object.

For example, run the following statement to verify that there are no statistics on the UnitPrice column of the Sales.SalesOrderDetail table:

```
DBCC SHOW_STATISTICS ('Sales.SalesOrderDetail', UnitPrice)
```
Listing 3-3.

If no statistics exists, which is the case for a fresh installation of the AdventureWorks database, you will receive the following error message:

```
Msg 2767, Level 16, State 1, Line 2
Could not locate statistics 'UnitPrice' in the system catalogs.
```

By then running the following query, the Query Optimizer will automatically create statistics on the UnitPrice column, which is used in the query predicate.

```
SELECT * FROM Sales.SalesOrderDetail
WHERE UnitPrice = 35
```
Listing 3-4.

Running the previous DBCC SHOW_STATISTICS statement again will now show a statistics object similar to the following output (displayed as text and edited to fit the page).

```
Name                         Updated               Rows   Rows Sampled Steps
-------------------------    --------------------  ------ ------------- ------
_WA_Sys_00000007_2645B050 Feb 24 2010  2:12PM 121317 110678           200


All density Average Length Columns
----------- -------------- -----------
0.003225806 8                UnitPrice


RANGE_HI_KEY RANGE_ROWS EQ_ROWS  DISTINCT_RANGE_ROWS AVG_RANGE_ROWS
------------ ---------- -------- ------------------- ---------------
1.374        0          144.3928 0                   1
2.29         34.27779   2779.8   0                   1
2.994        429.5555   342.3352 3                   1
3.975        34.27779   1        0                   18.33333
3.99         34.27779   2064.53  0                   1
4.611        146.0489   33.46852 3                   1
```

Listing 3-5.

The output is separated into three result sets called the header, the density vector and the histogram, all of which you can see above, although the header information has been truncated to fit onto the page. Let us look at the columns of the header using the previous statistics object example, bearing in mind that some of the columns I'll describe are not visible in Listing 3-5.

- **Name: _WA_Sys_00000007_2645B050**. This is the name of the statistics object, and will probably be different in your SQL Server instance. All automatically generated statistics have a name that starts with _WA_Sys. The 00000007 value is the column_id of the column which these statistics are based on, as can be seen on the sys.columns catalog, and 2645B050 is the hexadecimal equivalent of the object_id value of the table (which can be easily verified using the calculator program available on Windows). Reportedly, WA stands for Washington, the state of the United States where the SQL Server development team is located.

- **Updated: Feb 24 2010 2:12PM**. This is the date and time at which the statistics object was created or last updated.

- **Rows: 121317**. This is the number of rows that existed in the table when the statistics object was created or last updated.

- **Rows Sampled: 111078**. This is the number of rows sampled when the statistics object was created or last updated.

- **Steps: 200**. This is the number of steps of the histogram, which will be explained in the next major section.

- **Density: 0.07004219**. This density value is no longer used by the Query Optimizer and it is only included for backward compatibility.

- **Average key length: 8**. This is the average number of bytes for the columns of the statistics object.

- **String Index. NO**. This value indicates if the statistics object contains string statistics and the only choices are **YES** or **NO**; SQL Server does not provide additional details about the string statistics. String statistics contain the data distribution for string columns, and can help to estimate the cardinality of queries with **LIKE** conditions. As indicated before, string statistics are only created for the first column, and only when the column is of a string data type.

- **Filter Expression** and **Unfiltered Rows**. These columns will be explained in the filtered statistics section, later in the chapter.

Below the header you'll find the density vector, which includes a wealth of potentially useful density information and will be explained in the next section.

Density

To better explain the density vector, run the statement in Listing 3-6 to inspect the statistics of the existing index, `IX_SalesOrderDetail_ProductID`.

```
DBCC SHOW_STATISTICS ('Sales.SalesOrderDetail', IX_SalesOrderDetail_ProductID)
```
Listing 3-6.

This will display the following density vector, which shows the densities for the `ProductID` column, as well as a combination of columns `ProductID`, `SalesOrderID`, and then `ProductID`, `SalesOrderID` and `SalesOrderDetailID`.

```
All density   Average Length Columns
------------  -------------- ----------------------------------------
0.003759399   4              ProductID
8.242868E-06  8              ProductID, SalesOrderID
8.242868E-06  12             ProductID, SalesOrderID, SalesOrderDetailID
```
Listing 3-7.

Density, which is defined as 1 / "number of distinct values," is listed in the `All density` field, and it is calculated for each set of columns, forming a prefix for the columns in the statistics object. For example, the statistics object in Listing 3-7 was created for the columns `ProductID`, `SalesOrderID` and `SalesOrderDetailID`, and so the density vector will show three different density values: one for `ProductID`, another one for `ProductID` and `SalesOrderID` combined, and a third one for the combination of `ProductID`, `SalesOrderID`, and `SalesOrderDetailID`. The names of the analyzed columns will be displayed in the `Columns` field, and the `Average Length` column will show the average number of bytes for each density value. In the previous example, all the columns were defined using the `int` data type, so the average lengths for each of the density values will be 4, 8 and 12 bytes. Now that we've seen how density information is structured, let's take a look at how it's used.

Density information can be used to improve the Query Optimizer's estimates for **GROUP BY** operations, and on equality predicates where a value is unknown, as in the case of local variables. To see how this is done, let's consider, for example, the number of distinct values for `ProductID` on the `Sales.SalesOrderDetail` table: 266. Density can be calculated, as mentioned earlier, as 1 / "number of distinct values," which in this case would be 1 / 266, which is 0.003759399 as shown on the first density value on Listing 3-7.

So, the Query Optimizer can use the density information to estimate the cardinality of GROUP BY queries. GROUP BY queries can benefit from the estimated number of distinct values, and this information is already available in the density value. If you have this density information, then all you have to do is to find the estimated number of distinct values by calculating the reciprocal of the density value. For example, to estimate the cardinality of the following query using GROUP BY ProductID, we can calculate the reciprocal of the ProductID density shown in Listing 3-7. In this case, we have 1 / 0.003759399, which gives us 266, which is the estimated number of rows shown on the plan in Figure 3-1.

```
SELECT ProductID FROM Sales.SalesOrderDetail
GROUP BY ProductID
```
Listing 3-8.

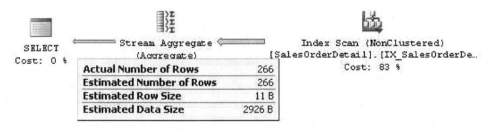

Figure 3-1:   Cardinality estimation example using a GROUP BY clause.

In a similar way, to test GROUP BY ProductID, SalesOrderID, we would need 1 / 8.242868E-06, which give us 121,317, which you can also verify by obtaining that query's graphical plan.

Listing 3-9 is an example of how the density can be used to estimate the cardinality of a query using local variables.

```
DECLARE @ProductID int
SET @ProductID = 921
SELECT ProductID FROM Sales.SalesOrderDetail
WHERE ProductID = @ProductID
```

Listing 3-9.

In this case, the Query Optimizer does not know the value of the `@ProductID` local variable at optimization time, so it is not able to use the histogram (which we'll discuss shortly) and will use the density information instead. The estimated number of rows is obtained using the density multiplied by the number of records in the table which, in our example, is 0.003759399 * 121317, or 456.079 as shown in Figure 3-2.

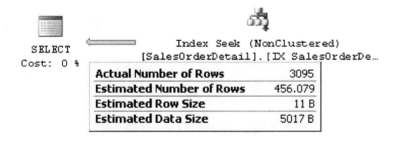

Actual Number of Rows	3095
Estimated Number of Rows	456.079
Estimated Row Size	11 B
Estimated Data Size	5017 B

Figure 3-2: Cardinality estimation example using a local variable.

Actually, since the Query Optimizer does not know the value of `@ProductID` at optimization time, the value of 921 in Listing 3-9 does not matter; any other value will give exactly the same estimated number of rows and execution plan. Finally, run this query with an inequality operator:

```
DECLARE @pid int = 897
SELECT * FROM Sales.SalesOrderDetail
WHERE ProductID < @pid
```

Listing 3-10.

Just as before, the value 897 does not matter; any other value will give you the same estimated number of rows and execution plan. However, this time the Query Optimizer is not able to use the density information and instead it is using the standard guess of 30% selectivity for inequality comparisons. That means that the estimated number of rows is always 30% of the total number of records for an inequality operator and, in this case, 30% of 121,317 is 36,395.1, as shown in Figure 3-3.

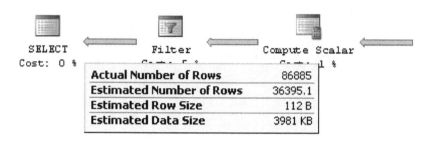

Actual Number of Rows	86885
Estimated Number of Rows	36395.1
Estimated Row Size	112 B
Estimated Data Size	3981 KB

Figure 3-3:   Cardinality estimation example using a 30% guess.

However, the use of local variables in a query limits the quality of the cardinality estimate when using the density information with equality operators. Worse, local variables result in no estimate at all when used with an inequality operator, which results in a guessed percentage. For this reason, local variables should be avoided in queries, and parameters or literals should be used instead. When parameters or literals *are* used, the Query Optimizer is able to use the histogram, which will provide better quality estimates than the density information on its own.

As it happens, the last section of the DBCC SHOW_STATISTICS output is the histogram, which I will now explain.

Histograms

In SQL Server, histograms are created only for the first column of a statistics object, and they compress the information of the distribution of values in those columns by partitioning that information into subsets called **buckets** or **steps**. The maximum number of steps in a histogram is 200, but even if the input has 200 or more unique values, a histogram may still have less than 200 steps. To build the histogram, SQL Server finds the unique values in the column and tries to capture the most frequent ones using a variation of the maxdiff algorithm, so that the most statistically significant information is preserved. Maxdiff is one of the available histograms whose purpose is to accurately represent the distribution of data values in relational databases.

To see how the histogram is used, run the following statement to display the current statistics of the `IX_SalesOrderDetail_ProductID` index on the `Sales.SalesOrderDetail` table:

```
DBCC SHOW_STATISTICS ('Sales.SalesOrderDetail', IX_SalesOrderDetail_ProductID)
```

Listing 3-11.

Both the multi-column index and statistics objects include the columns `ProductID`, `SalesOrderID`, and `SalesOrderDetailID`, but since the histogram is only for the first column, this data is only available for the `ProductID` column.

Next, I will show you some examples of how the histogram may be used to estimate the cardinality of some simple predicates. Let's take a look at a section of the histogram, as shown in the output in Listing 3-12.

```
RANGE_HI_KEY RANGE_ROWS EQ_ROWS DISTINCT_RANGE_ROWS AVG_RANGE_ROWS

------------ ---------- ------- -------------------- --------------
826          0          305     0                    1
831          110        198     3                    36.66667
832          0          256     0                    1
```

Listing 3-12.

RANGE_HI_KEY is the upper boundary of a histogram step; the value 826 is the upper boundary for the first step displayed, and 831 is the upper boundary for the second step shown. This means that the second step may contain only values from 827 to 831.

With that in mind, and to better understand the rest of the histogram structure and how the histogram information was aggregated, run the following query to obtain the real number of records for ProductIDs 827 to 831, and we'll compare them against the histogram.

```
SELECT ProductID, COUNT(*) AS Total
FROM Sales.SalesOrderDetail
WHERE ProductID BETWEEN 827 AND 831
GROUP BY ProductID
```

Listing 3-13.

This produces the following result:

```
ProductID Total
--------- -----------
827       31
828       46
830       33
831       198
```

Listing 3-14.

Going back to the histogram, EQ_ROWS is the estimated number of rows whose column value equals RANGE_HI_KEY. So, in our example, for the RANGE_HI_KEY value of 831, EQ_ROWS shows 198, which we know is also the actual number of existing records for ProductID 831.

RANGE_ROWS is the estimated number of rows whose column value falls inside the range of the step, *excluding* the upper boundary. In our example, this is the number of records with values from 827 to 830 (831, the upper boundary or RANGE_HI_KEY, is excluded). The histogram shows 110 records and we could obtain the same value by getting the sum of 31 records for ProductID 827, 46 records for ProductID 828, 0 records for ProductID 829, and 33 records for ProductID 830.

DISTINCT_RANGE_ROWS is the estimated number of rows with a distinct column value inside this range, once again excluding the upper boundary. In our example, we have records for three distinct values: 827, 828, and 830, so DISTINCT_RANGE_ROWS is 3. There are no records for ProductID 829, and 831, which is the upper boundary, is again excluded.

Finally, AVG_RANGE_ROWS is the average number of rows per distinct value, excluding the upper boundary, and it is simply calculated as RANGE_ROWS / DISTINCT_RANGE_ROWS. In our example, we have a total of 110 records for 3 DISTINCT_RANGE_ROWS, which gives us 110 / 3 = 36.6667, also shown in the second step of the histogram shown previously.

Now let's see how the histogram is used to estimate the selectivity of some queries. Let us see the first query:

```
SELECT * FROM Sales.SalesOrderDetail
WHERE ProductID = 831
```

Listing 3-15.

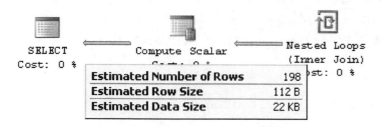

Figure 3-4:   Cardinality estimation example using a RANGE_HI_KEY value.

Since 831 is the RANGE_HI_KEY on the second step of the histogram shown in Listing 3-12, the Query Optimizer will use the EQ_ROWS value (the estimated number of rows whose column value equals RANGE_HI_KEY) directly, and the estimated number of rows will be 198, as shown on Figure 3-4.

Now run the same query, with the value set to 828. This time, the value is inside the range of the second step but is not a RANGE_HI_KEY, so the Query Optimizer uses the value calculated for AVG_RANGE_ROWS (the average number of rows per distinct value), which is 36.6667 as shown in the histogram. The plan is shown in Figure 3-5 and, unsurprisingly, we get the same estimated number of rows for any of the other values in the range (except for the RANGE_HI_KEY, obviously). This also includes 829, even when there are no records for this ProductID value.

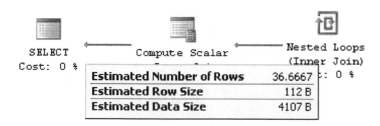

Figure 3-5:   Cardinality estimation example using an AVG_RANGE_ROWS value.

Let's now use an inequality operator and try to find the records with a **ProductID** less than 714. Since this requires all the records, both inside the range of a step and the upper boundary, we need to calculate the sum of the values of both the **RANGE_ROWS** and the **EQ_ROWS** columns for steps 1 through 7 as shown in the histogram below, which give us a total of 13,223 rows.

RANGE_HI_KEY	RANGE_ROWS	EQ_ROWS	DISTINCT_RANGE_ROWS	AVG_RANGE_ROWS
707	0	3083	0	1
708	0	3007	0	1
709	0	188	0	1
710	0	44	0	1
711	0	3090	0	1
712	0	3382	0	1
713	0	429	0	1
714	0	1218	0	1
715	0	1635	0	1

Listing 3-16.

This is the query in question, and the estimated number of rows is shown on the execution plan in Figure 3-6.

```
SELECT * FROM Sales.SalesOrderDetail
WHERE ProductID < 714
```

Listing 3-17.

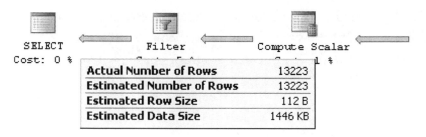

Actual Number of Rows	13223
Estimated Number of Rows	13223
Estimated Row Size	112 B
Estimated Data Size	1446 KB

Figure 3-6:   Cardinality estimation example using an inequality operator.

Let's now test a query with an AND'ed predicate (this example shows statistics as estimated in SQL Server 2008; statistics for SQL Server 2008 R2 will have minimal differences for a default sample).

```
SELECT * FROM Sales.SalesOrderDetail
WHERE ProductID = 870 AND OrderQty = 1
```

Listing 3-18.

SQL Server will use the histograms of two distinct statistics objects here, one for each predicate clause. We can use one histogram to obtain the estimated number of records for ProductID = 870, and the second histogram to obtain the estimated number of records for OrderQty = 1. Requesting ProductID = 870 AND OrderQty = 1 will return the intersection between both sets of records, so we should multiply the *selectivity* of both clauses to obtain this value.

If you obtain the estimated number of rows for the predicate ProductID = 870 alone, as explained before, you will get 4,688 rows. For a table with 121,317 records, this corresponds to a selectivity of 4,688 / 121,317, or 0.03864256. In the same way, the estimated number of rows for the predicate OrderQty = 1 alone is 68,024 rows, which corresponds to a selectivity of 68,024 / 121,317, or 0.56071284.

In order to get the intersection of these sets, we need to multiply the selectivity values of both predicate clauses, 0.03864256 * 0.56071284 to get 0.0216673795624704. Finally, the calculated selectivity is multiplied by the number of records to give the estimated number of records as 0.0216673795624704 * 121,317, or 2,628.62, which is the value shown in the graphical plan in Figure 3-7.

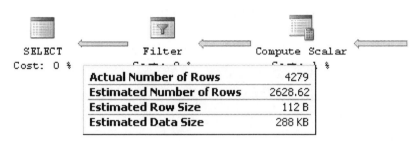

Actual Number of Rows	4279
Estimated Number of Rows	2628.62
Estimated Row Size	112 B
Estimated Data Size	288 KB

Figure 3-7:   Cardinality estimation example using an AND'ed predicate.

It is also worth noticing that if these two columns, `ProductID` and `OrderQty`, were correlated (which is not the case in this example), then this method to estimate the cardinality would be incorrect. Two methods to help with correlated columns are using multi-column statistics, as mentioned before, and filtered statistics, which will be explained later in this chapter.

Finally, let's test the same query with an OR'ed predicate to see how the information revealed by the histogram will be helpful.

```
SELECT * FROM Sales.SalesOrderDetail
WHERE ProductID = 870 OR OrderQty = 1
```
Listing 3-19.

By definition, an OR'ed predicate is the union of the sets of rows of both clauses, without duplicates. That is, this should be the rows estimated for `ProductID = 870` plus the rows estimated for `OrderQty = 1`, but if there are any rows that may belong to both sets, then they should be included only once. As indicated in the previous example, the estimated number of rows for the predicate `ProductID = 870` alone, is 4,688 rows, and the estimated number of rows for the predicate `OrderQty = 1` alone is 68,024 rows.

The estimated number of records that belong to both sets is the `AND`'ed predicate we saw previously: 2,628.62 rows. So, the estimated number of rows for the `OR`'ed predicate is 4,688 + 68,024 – 2,628.62, or 70083.4, as shown in the execution plan in Figure 3-8.

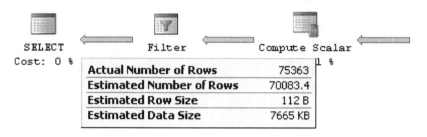

SELECT	Filter	Compute Scalar
Cost: 0 %		l %

Actual Number of Rows	75363
Estimated Number of Rows	70083.4
Estimated Row Size	112 B
Estimated Data Size	7665 KB

Figure 3-8: Cardinality estimation example using an OR'ed predicate.

Statistics Maintenance

As mentioned already, the Query Optimizer will, by default, automatically update statistics when they are out of date. Statistics can also be updated with the **UPDATE STATISTICS** statement which you can schedule to run as a job during your database maintenance window. Another statement commonly used, **sp_updatestats**, also runs **UPDATE STATISTICS** behind the scenes.

There are two important benefits of updating statistics in a maintenance job. The first is that your queries will use updated statistics without having to wait for the automatic update of statistics to be completed, avoiding delays in the optimization of your queries (although asynchronous statistics updates can also be used to partially help with this problem). The second benefit is that you can use a bigger sample than the Query Optimizer will use, or you can even scan the entire table. This can give you better quality statistics for big tables, especially for those where data is not randomly distributed in their data pages. Manually updating statistics can also be a benefit after operations such as data loads, that update large amounts of data, are performed.

On the other hand, also note that the update of statistics will cause a recompiling of plans already in the plan cache which are using these statistics, so you may not want to do this too often, either.

An additional consideration for manually updating statistics in a maintenance job is how they relate to index rebuild maintenance jobs, which also update the index statistics. Keep the following items in mind when combining maintenance jobs for both indexes and statistics, remembering that there are both index and non-index column statistics, and that index operations obviously may impact only the first of these.

- **Rebuilding an index**, for example by using the ALTER INDEX ... REBUILD statement, will also update index statistics by scanning all the rows in the table, which is the equivalent of using UPDATE STATISTICS WITH FULLSCAN. Rebuilding indexes does not update any column statistics.

- **Reorganizing an index**, for example using the ALTER INDEX ... REORGANIZE statement, does not update any statistics, not even index statistics.

- **By default**, the UPDATE STATISTICS statement updates both index and column statistics. Using the INDEX option will update index statistics only, and using the COLUMNS option will update non-indexed column statistics only.

So, depending on your maintenance jobs and scripts, several scenarios can exist. The simplest maintenance plan is if you want to rebuild all the indexes and update all the statistics. As mentioned before, if you rebuild all your indexes, then all the index statistics will also be automatically updated by scanning all the rows on the table. Then you just need to update your non-indexed column statistics by running UPDATE STATISTICS WITH FULLSCAN, COLUMNS. Since one job updates only index statistics, and the second one updates only column statistics, it does not matter which one is executed first.

Of course, more complicated maintenance plans can exist, for example, when indexes are rebuilt or reorganized depending on their fragmentation level. A good starting point to do this is to use the `avg_fragmentation_in_percent` column and the index fragmentation thresholds as defined on the Books Online entry for the `sys.dm_db_index_physical_stats` dynamic management function. You should keep in mind the items mentioned above, so that you can avoid problems like updating the index statistics twice, as could occur when both index rebuild and update statistics operations are performed. You could also avoid discarding work previously performed, for example, when you rebuild the indexes of a table (which also updates statistics by scanning the entire table), and later running a job updating the statistics with a default or smaller sample.

Let me show you how these commands work, with some examples. Create a new table `dbo.SalesOrderDetail`:

```
SELECT * INTO dbo.SalesOrderDetail
FROM sales.SalesOrderDetail
```
Listing 3-20.

The next query uses the `sys.stats` catalog view to show that there are no statistics objects for the new table:

```
SELECT name, auto_created, stats_date(object_id, stats_id) AS update_date
FROM sys.stats
WHERE object_id = object_id('dbo.SalesOrderDetail')
```
Listing 3-21.

Now run the following query:

```
SELECT * FROM dbo.SalesOrderDetail
WHERE SalesOrderID = 43670 AND OrderQty = 1
```

Listing 3-22.

Use the previous **sys.stats** query from Listing 3-21 to verify that two statistics objects were created, one for the **SalesOrderID** column, and a second for the **OrderQty** column. Now create the following index, and run the **sys.stats** query again to verify that a new statistics object for the **ProductID** column has been created.

```
CREATE INDEX IX_ProductID ON dbo.SalesOrderDetail(ProductID)
```

Listing 3-23.

This will be the output of the **sys.stats** query so far:

```
name                      auto_created update_date
------------------------- ------------ -----------------------
_WA_Sys_00000004_76EBA2E9 1            2010-03-01 14:17:44.610
_WA_Sys_00000001_76EBA2E9 1            2010-03-01 14:17:44.770
IX_ProductID              0            2010-03-01 14:19:00.607
```

Listing 3-24.

Notice how the value of the **auto_created** column, which indicates if the statistics were created by the Query Optimizer, is 0 for the **IX_ProductID** statistics object. Run the next command to update just the column statistics:

```
UPDATE STATISTICS dbo.SalesOrderDetail WITH FULLSCAN, COLUMNS
```

Listing 3-25.

You can validate that only the column statistics were updated, by comparing the **update_date** column with the previous output. The **update_date** column uses the **STATS_DATE** function to display the last point in time when the statistics were updated, as is shown on the following output:

```
name                    auto_created update_date
----------------------- ------------ -----------------------
_WA_Sys_00000004_76EBA2E9  1            2010-03-01 14:21:25.850
_WA_Sys_00000001_76EBA2E9  1            2010-03-01 14:21:25.940
IX_ProductID               0            2010-03-01 14:19:00.607
```

Listing 3-26.

This command will do the same for just the index statistics:

```
UPDATE STATISTICS dbo.SalesOrderDetail WITH FULLSCAN, INDEX
```

Listing 3-27.

... and these commands will update both the index and column statistics:

```
UPDATE STATISTICS dbo.SalesOrderDetail WITH FULLSCAN
UPDATE STATISTICS dbo.SalesOrderDetail WITH FULLSCAN, ALL
```

Listing 3-28.

As mentioned earlier, if you run the **sys.stats** query after each of the next two queries, you'll see how an **ALTER INDEX REBUILD** statement only updates index statistics:

```
ALTER INDEX ix_ProductID ON dbo.SalesOrderDetail REBUILD
```

Listing 3-29.

... and you can verify that reorganizing an index does not update any statistics:

```
ALTER INDEX ix_ProductID  on dbo.SalesOrderDetail REORGANIZE
```

Listing 3-30.

Finally, for good house-keeping, remove the table you have just created:

```
DROP TABLE dbo.SalesOrderDetail
```

Listing 3-31.

Statistics on Computed Columns

Another interesting step performed during query optimization is the automatic matching of computed columns. Although computed columns have been available in previous versions of SQL Server, the automatic matching feature was only introduced with SQL Server 2005. In this section, I will show you how this feature works, and explain how computed columns can help to improve the performance of your queries.

A problem faced by some queries using scalar expressions is that they usually cannot benefit from column statistics and, without statistics, the Query Optimizer will use the 30% selectivity guess on inequality comparisons, which may produce inefficient execution plans. A solution to this problem is the use of computed columns, as SQL Server can automatically create and update statistics on these columns. The great benefit of this solution is that you don't need to specify the name of the computed column in your queries for SQL Server to use its statistics. The Query Optimizer automatically matches the computed column definition to an existing scalar expression in a query, so your applications do not need to be changed.

To see an example, run this query, which creates the plan shown in Figure 3-9:

```
SELECT * FROM Sales.SalesOrderDetail
WHERE OrderQty * UnitPrice > 10000
```

Listing 3-32.

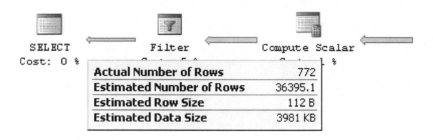

Actual Number of Rows	772
Estimated Number of Rows	36395.1
Estimated Row Size	112 B
Estimated Data Size	3981 KB

Figure 3-9:   Cardinality estimation example using a 30% guess.

The estimated number of rows is 36,395.1, which is 30% of the total number of rows, 121,317, although the query returns only 772 records. SQL Server is obviously using a selectivity guess, as it cannot estimate the selectivity of the expression OrderQty * UnitPrice > 10000.

Now create a computed column:

```
ALTER TABLE Sales.SalesOrderDetail
ADD cc AS OrderQty * UnitPrice
```

Listing 3-33.

Run the previous query in Listing 3-32 again, and note that, this time, the estimated number of rows has changed and is close to the actual number of rows returned by the query, as shown in Figure 3-10 (this plan shows the estimated number of rows as in SQL Server 2008; statistics for SQL Server 2008 R2 will have minimal differences for a default sample). You can optionally test replacing the 10,000 with some other values, like 10, 100, 1,000, or 5,000, and compare the actual and the estimated number of rows returned.

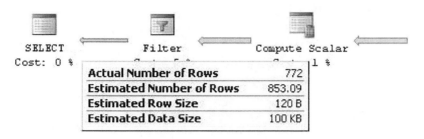

Actual Number of Rows	772
Estimated Number of Rows	853.09
Estimated Row Size	120 B
Estimated Data Size	100 KB

Figure 3-10: Cardinality estimation example using computed columns.

Note that creating the computed column does not create statistics; these statistics are created the first time that the query is optimized, and you can run the next query to display the information about the statistics objects for the `Sales.SalesOrderDetail` table:

```
SELECT * FROM sys.stats
WHERE object_id = object_id('Sales.SalesOrderDetail')
```
Listing 3-34.

The newly created statistics object will most likely be at the end of the list. Copy the name of the object, and use the following command to display the details about the statistics object (I've used the name of my local object, but you should replace that as appropriate). You can also use "cc" as the name of the object to get the same results. The "cc" column should be shown on the Columns field in the density section.

```
DBCC SHOW_STATISTICS ('Sales.SalesOrderDetail', _WA_Sys_00000013_2645B050)
```
Listing 3-35.

Unfortunately, for automatic matching to work, the expression must be exactly the same as the computed column definition. So, if I change the query to `UnitPrice * OrderQty`, instead of `OrderQty * UnitPrice`, the execution plan will show an estimated number of rows of 30% again, as this query will demonstrate:

```
SELECT * FROM Sales.SalesOrderDetail
WHERE UnitPrice * OrderQty > 10000
```
Listing 3-36.

Finally, drop the created computed column:

```
ALTER TABLE Sales.SalesOrderDetail
DROP COLUMN cc
```
Listing 3-37.

Filtered Statistics

Filtered statistics are statistics created on a subset of records in a table. Filtered statistics are automatically created when filtered indexes are created, but they can also be created manually by specifying a **WHERE** clause on the **CREATE STATISTICS** statement. As you might imagine, filtered statistics can help on queries accessing specific subsets of data. They can also be useful in situations like correlated columns, especially when one of these columns has a small number of unique values, and you can create multiple filtered statistics for each one of these distinct values. As shown in the histogram section previously, when using multiple predicates, SQL Server assumes that each clause in a query is independent and, if the columns used in this query were correlated, then the cardinality estimation would be incorrect. Filtered statistics may also help on huge tables where a large number of unique values are not accurately represented in the 200-step limitation currently enforced on histograms.

Next, I will show you how you can use filtered statistics to help in a problem with correlated columns. Running the following query will correctly estimate the number of rows to be 93:

```
SELECT * FROM Person.Address
WHERE City = 'Los Angeles'
```

Listing 3-38.

In the same way, running the next query will correctly estimate 4,564 rows:

```
SELECT * FROM Person.Address
WHERE StateProvinceID = 9
```

Listing 3-39.

However, since `StateProvinceID` 9 corresponds to the state of California (which you can verify by looking at the `Person.StateProvince` table) it is possible for somebody to run this query, which in this case will show a less precise estimate of 21.6403, as shown in the plan in Figure 3-11.

```
SELECT * FROM Person.Address
WHERE City = 'Los Angeles' AND StateProvinceID = 9
```

Listing 3-40.

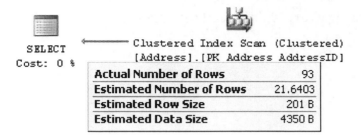

Actual Number of Rows	93
Estimated Number of Rows	21.6403
Estimated Row Size	201 B
Estimated Data Size	4350 B

Figure 3-11: Cardinality estimate with the independence assumption.

Because of the assumption of independence, SQL Server will multiply the cardinality of both predicates, which was explained earlier in this chapter. The calculation, abbreviated as (93 * 4,564) / 19,614, will give us the value 21.6403 shown in the previous plan (19,614 is the total number of rows in the table).

However, the assumption of independence is incorrect in this example, as the columns are statistically correlated. To help with this problem, you can create a filtered statistics object for the state of California, as shown in the next statement.

```
CREATE STATISTICS california
ON Person.Address(City)
WHERE StateProvinceID = 9
```

Listing 3-41.

Clearing the cache and running the previous query again will now give a better estimate, as shown on the following plan:

```
DBCC FREEPROCCACHE
GO
SELECT * FROM Person.Address
WHERE City = 'Los Angeles' AND StateProvinceID = 9
```

Listing 3-42.

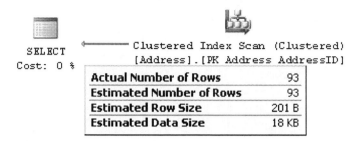

Figure 3-12: Cardinality estimate with filtered statistics.

Let us now inspect the filtered statistics object by running the following statement:

```
DBCC SHOW_STATISTICS('Person.Address', california)
WITH STAT_HEADER
```

Listing 3-43.

This will show the following output, (edited here to fit the page):

```
Name        Rows   Rows Sampled  Filter Expression         Unfiltered Rows
----------- -----  ------------- ------------------------- ----------------
california  4564   4564          ([StateProvinceID]=(9))   19614
```

Listing 3-44.

Notice that the filter definition is shown on the Filter Expression field, and that the Unfiltered Rows field shows the total number of records on the table when the filtered statistics were created. Also note that, this time, the Rows column number is *less* than the total number of rows in the table, and corresponds to the number of records that satisfied the filter predicate when the statistics object was created. The filter definition can also be seen on the `filter_definition` column of the `sys.stats` catalog view.

Finally, drop the statistics object you have just created, by running the following statement:

```
DROP STATISTICS Person.Address.california
```

Listing 3-45.

Cardinality Estimation Errors

Cardinality estimation errors can lead to the Query Optimizer making poor choices as to how best to execute a query and, therefore, to badly performing execution plans. Fortunately, you can easily check if you have cardinality estimation errors by comparing the estimated against the actual number of rows, as shown on graphical or XML execution plans, or by using the **SET STATISTICS PROFILE** statement. In the next query, I'll show you how to use the **SET STATISTICS PROFILE** statement with one of our previous examples where SQL Server is making a blind guess regarding the selectivity of certain columns:

```
SET STATISTICS PROFILE ON
GO
SELECT * FROM Sales.SalesOrderDetail
WHERE OrderQty * UnitPrice > 10000
GO
SET STATISTICS PROFILE OFF
GO
```

Listing 3-46.

This is the resulting output, with the **EstimateRows** column manually moved just after the **Rows** column, and edited to fit the page:

```
Rows    EstimateRows Executes StmtText
------  ------------ -------- ----------------------------------------------
 772    36395.1      1        SELECT * FROM [Sales].[SalesOrderDetail]
 772    36395.1      1         |--Filter(WHERE:([AdventureWorks] .[Sa
   0    121317       0          |--Compute Scalar(DEFINE:(([Advent
   0    121317       0            |--Compute Scalar(DEFINE:(([A
121317  121317       1             |--Clustered Index Scan
```

Listing 3-47.

Using this output, you can easily compare the actual number of rows, shown on the **Rows** column, against the estimated number of records, as shown on the **EstimateRows** column, for each operator in the plan.

Because each operator relies on previous operations for its input, cardinality estimation errors can propagate exponentially throughout the query plan. For example, a cardinality estimation error on a Filter operator can impact the cardinality estimation of all the other operators in the plan that consume the data produced by that operator. If your query is not performing well and you find cardinality estimation errors, check for problems like missing or out-of-date statistics, very small samples being used, correlation between columns, use of scalar expressions, guessing selectivity issues, and so on.

Recommendations to help with these issues have been provided throughout this chapter and include things like using the auto-create and auto-update statistics default configurations, updating statistics using **WITH FULLSCAN**, avoiding local variables in queries, using computed columns, and considering multi-column or filtered statistics, among other things. That's a fairly long list, but it should help convince you that you are already armed with pragmatically useful information.

Some SQL Server features, such as table variables, do not use statistics, so you might want to consider using a similar feature like temporary tables if you're having performance problems related to cardinality estimation errors. In addition, for complex queries that are not performing well because of cardinality estimation errors, you may want to consider partitioning the query into several steps while storing the intermediate results in temporary tables. This will allow SQL Server to create statistics on the intermediate results, which will help the Query Optimizer to produce a better execution plan.

UPDATE STATISTICS with ROWCOUNT, PAGECOUNT

In this section I will show you the undocumented ROWCOUNT and PAGECOUNT options of the UPDATE STATISTICS statement, which can help you in cases where you want to see which execution plans would be generated for huge tables (with millions of records), but then test those plans in small, or even empty, tables. As you can imagine, these options can be helpful for testing in some scenarios where you may not want to spent time or disk space creating big tables.

By using this method you are essentially tricking the Query Optimizer, as it will generate execution plans using cardinality estimations which are made as if the table really had millions of records, even if your table is actually tiny. Note that this option, available since SQL Server 2005, only helps in creating the *execution plan* for your queries. Actually running the query will use the real data in your test table which will, of course, execute faster than a table with millions of records.

Using these UPDATE STATISTICS options does not change the table statistics, only the counters for the numbers of rows and pages of a table and, as I will show shortly, the Query Optimizer uses this information to estimate the cardinality of queries. Finally, before we look at examples, keep in mind that these are undocumented and unsupported options, and should not be used in a production environment.

So, let's see an example. Run the following query to create a new table on the **Adven-tureWorks** database:

```
SELECT * INTO dbo.Address
FROM Person.Address
```
Listing 3-48.

Inspect the number of rows by running the following queries; they should show 19,614 rows:

```
SELECT * FROM sys.partitions
WHERE object_id = object_id('dbo.Address')
```
Listing 3-49.

```
SELECT * FROM sys.dm_db_partition_stats
WHERE object_id = object_id('dbo.Address')
```
Listing 3-50.

Now run the following query, and inspect the graphical execution plan:

```
SELECT * FROM dbo.Address
WHERE City = 'London'
```
Listing 3-51.

Running this query will create a new statistics object for the **City** column, and will show the plan in Figure 3-13. Note that the estimated number of rows is 434, and it's using a simple Table Scan operator.

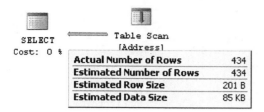

Figure 3-13: Cardinality estimation example using a small table.

We can discover where the Query Optimizer is getting the estimated number of rows by inspecting the statistics object. Run this query to see the name of the statistics object ...

```
SELECT * FROM sys.stats
WHERE object_id = object_id('dbo.Address')
```

Listing 3-52.

... and then use the displayed statistics object name in the following statement (the name may be different in your case).

```
DBCC SHOW_STATISTICS ('dbo.Address', _WA_Sys_00000004_46136164)
```

Listing 3-53.

A fragment of the histogram is shown next.

RANGE_HI_KEY	RANGE_ROWS	EQ_ROWS	DISTINCT_RANGE_ROWS	AVG_RANGE_ROWS
Lincoln Acres	0	102	0	1
London	32	434	2	16
Long Beach	0	97	0	1
Los Angeles	2	93	2	1

Listing 3-54.

By looking at the histogram, you can find the value 434 on EQ_ROWS for the RANGE_HI_
KEY value "London."

Now run the following UPDATE STATISTICS WITH ROWCOUNT, PAGECOUNT statement
(you can specify any other value for ROWCOUNT and PAGECOUNT):

```
UPDATE STATISTICS dbo.Address WITH ROWCOUNT = 1000000, PAGECOUNT = 100000
```

Listing 3-55.

If you inspect the number of rows from sys.partitions or sys.dm_db_parti-
tion_stats again, as shown previously, it will now show 1,000,000 rows (sys.dm_db_
partition_stats also shows the new number of pages). Clear the plan cache and run
the query again.

```
DBCC FREEPROCCACHE
GO
SELECT * FROM dbo.Address
WHERE City = 'London'
```

Listing 3-56.

Note that the estimated number of rows has changed from 434 to 22,127.1, as shown on
Figure 3-14, and that a different plan was generated using this new cardinality estimation;
this time, the Query Optimizer decided to create a parallel plan.

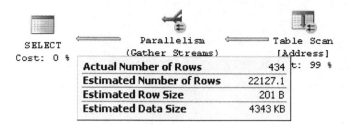

Figure 3-14: Cardinality estimation using ROWCOUNT and PAGECOUNT.

However, if you look at the statistics object again, using **DBCC SHOW_STATISTICS** as shown before, you'll see that the histogram has not changed. One way to obtain the estimated number of rows shown in the new execution plan is by calculating the percentage (or fraction) of rows for the value "London" from the statistics sample which, in this case, is 19,614, as will be shown in the header of the statistics object referred to in Listing 3-54. So the fraction is 434 / 19,614, or 0.022127052. Next, we apply the same percentage to the new "current" number of rows, which results in 1,000,000 * 0.022127052, and we get 22,127.1, which is the estimated number of rows displayed in the plan in Figure 3-14.

Finally, drop the table you just created:

```
DROP TABLE dbo.Address
```

Listing 3-57.

Cost Estimation

As we've established, the quality of the execution plans the Query Optimizer generates is directly related to the accuracy of its costing estimates. Even when the Query Optimizer is able to enumerate low cost plans, an incorrect cost estimation may result in the Query Optimizer choosing inefficient plans, which can negatively impact the performance of your database. During query optimization, the Query Optimizer explores many candidate plans, estimates their cost, and then selects the most efficient one. So, in addition to being accurate, cost estimation must also be efficient, since it is used multiple times during the query optimization process.

Costs are estimated for any partial or complete plan; cost computation is done per operator, and the total plan cost is the sum of the costs of all the operators in that plan. The cost of each operator depends on its algorithm and the estimated number of records it returns, and some operators, such as Sort or Hash Join, also consider the available memory in the system. A high level overview of the cost of the algorithms for some of the most used operators was included in *Chapter 2, The Execution Engine*.

So, each operator has an associated CPU cost, and some of them will also have some I/O cost, and the cost of the operator as a whole is the sum of these costs. An operator like a Clustered Index Scan has both CPU and I/O costs, whereas some other operators, like Stream Aggregate, will only have a CPU cost. Since Microsoft does not publish how these costs are calculated, I will show you a very basic example of how the cost of a plan is estimated.

To show this in an example, let's look at the largest table in the **AdventureWorks** database. Run the following query and look at the estimated CPU and I/O costs for the Clustered Index Scan operator, as shown in Figure 3-15:

```
SELECT * FROM Sales.SalesOrderDetail
WHERE LineTotal = 35
```

Listing 3-58.

Clustered Index Scan (Clustered)	
Scanning a clustered index, entirely or only a range.	
Physical Operation	Clustered Index Scan
Logical Operation	Clustered Index Scan
Actual Number of Rows	121317
Estimated I/O Cost	0.916458
Estimated CPU Cost	0.133606
Number of Executions	1
Estimated Number of Executions	1
Estimated Operator Cost	1.05006 (93%)
Estimated Subtree Cost	1.05006
Estimated Number of Rows	121317
Estimated Row Size	95 B
Actual Rebinds	0
Actual Rewinds	0
Ordered	False
Node ID	3
Object	
[AdventureWorks].[Sales].[SalesOrderDetail].	
[PK_SalesOrderDetail_SalesOrderID_SalesOrderDetailID]	

Figure 3-15:   Clustered Index Scan operator properties.

Note that, in an older version of SQL Server, the cost used to mean the estimated time in seconds that a query would take to execute on a specific hardware configuration, but currently this value is meaningless as an objective unit of measurement, and should not be interpreted as one.

For a Clustered Index Scan operator, I observed that the CPU cost is 0.0001581 for the first record, plus 0.0000011 for any additional record after that. Because, in this specific case, we have an estimated 121,317 records, we can calculate 0.0001581 + 0.0000011 * (121317 – 1), which comes to 0.133606, which is the value shown as `Estimated CPU Cost`. In a similar way, I noticed that the minimum I/O cost is 0.003125 for the first database page, and then it grows in increments of 0.00074074 for every additional page. Since this operator scans the entire table, I can use the query in Listing 3-59 to find the number of database pages (which turns out to be 1,234).

```
SELECT in_row_data_page_count, row_count
FROM sys.dm_db_partition_stats
WHERE object_id = object_id('Sales.SalesOrderDetail')
AND index_id = 1
```

Listing 3-59.

In this case I have 0.003125 + 0.00074074 * (1234 – 1), which comes to 0.916458, which is the value shown as `Estimated I/O Cost`.

Finally, we add both costs, 0.133606 + 0.916458, to get 1.05006, which is the total estimated cost of the operator. In the same way, adding the cost of all the operators will give the total cost of the plan. In this case, the cost of the Clustered Index Scan (1.05006) plus the cost of the first Compute Scalar operator (0.01214), the second Compute Scalar operator (0.01213), and the cost of the Filter operator (0.0582322), will give the total cost of the plan: 1.13256, as shown on Figure 3-16.

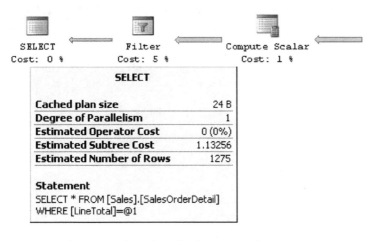

Figure 3-16: Execution plan displaying total cost.

Summary

In this chapter, we have seen how statistics are used by SQL Server to estimate the cardinality as well as the cost of operators and execution plans. The most important elements of a statistics object, namely the histogram, the density information, and string statistics, were introduced and explained. Examples of how to use histograms were shown, including queries with equality and inequality operators and both AND'ed and OR'ed predicates. The use of density information was shown in GROUP BY operations, and in cases when the Query Optimizer is not able to use a histogram, such as in the case of local variables.

Maintenance of statistics was also explained, with some emphasis on how to proactively update statistics to avoid delays during query optimization, and how to improve the quality of statistics by scanning the entire table instead of a default sample. We also discussed how to detect cardinality estimation errors, which can negatively impact the quality of your execution plans, and we looked at recommendations on how to fix them.

Chapter 4: Index Selection

Index selection is one of the most important techniques used in query optimization. By using the right indexes, SQL Server can speed up your queries and dramatically improve the performance of your applications. In this chapter, I will show you how SQL Server selects indexes, how you can use this knowledge to provide better indexes, and how you can verify your execution plans to make sure these indexes are correctly used.

This chapter also includes sections about the Database Engine Tuning Advisor and the Missing Indexes feature, which will show how you can use the Query Optimizer itself to provide index tuning recommendations. However, it is important to emphasize that, no matter what index recommendations these tools give, it is ultimately up to the database administrator or developer to do their own index analysis, and finally decide which of these recommendations to implement. Also, since we'll be covering these tools mainly from the point of view of the Query Optimizer, you should use Books Online to obtain more in-depth information regarding using these features.

Finally, the `sys.dm_db_index_usage_stats` DMV will be introduced as a tool to identify existing indexes which your queries may not be using. Indexes that are not being used will provide no benefit to your databases, but *will* use valuable disk space and slow your update operations, and so they should be considered for removal.

Introduction

As mentioned in *Chapter 2*, *The Execution Engine*, SQL Server can use indexes to perform seek and scan operations. Indexes can be used to speed up the execution of a query by quickly finding records without performing table scans; by delivering all the columns requested by the query without accessing the base table (i.e. covering the query, which

I'll return to in a moment), or by providing sorted order, like in queries with GROUP BY, DISTINCT or ORDER BY clauses.

Part of the Query Optimizer's job is to determine if an index can be used to evaluate a predicate in a query. This is basically a comparison between an index key and a constant or variable. In addition, the Query Optimizer needs to determine if the index covers the query; that is, if the index contains all the columns required by the query (referred to as a "covering index"). It needs to confirm this because, as you'll hopefully remember, a non-clustered index usually contains only a subset of the columns of the table.

SQL Server can also consider using more than one index, and joining them to cover all the columns required by the query (index intersection). If it's not possible to cover all of the columns required by the query, it may need to access the base table, which could be a clustered index or a heap, to obtain the remaining columns. This is called a bookmark lookup operation (which could be a Key Lookup or a RID Lookup, as explained in Chapter 2). However, since a bookmark lookup requires random I/O, which is a very expensive operation, its usage can be effective only for a relatively small number of records.

Also keep in mind that, although one or more indexes *can* be used, it does not mean that they will finally be selected in an execution plan, as this is always a cost-based decision. So, after creating an index, make sure you verify that the index is, in fact, used in a plan (and, of course, that your query is performing better, which is probably the primary reason why you are defining an index). An index that it is not being used by any query will just take up valuable disk space, and may negatively impact the performance of update operations without providing any benefit. It is also possible that an index, which *was* useful when it was originally created, is no longer used by any query. This could be as a result of changes in the database, the data, or even the query itself. To help you avoid this frustrating situation, the last section in this chapter will show you how you can identify which indexes are no longer being used by any of your queries.

The Mechanics of Index Selection

In a seek operation, SQL Server navigates throughout the B-tree index to quickly find the required records without the need for an index or table scan. This is similar to using an index at the end of a book to find a topic quickly, instead of reading the entire book. Once the first record has been found, SQL Server can then scan the index leaf level forward or backward to find additional records. Both equality and inequality operators can be used in a predicate, including =, <, >, <=, >=, <>, !=, !<, !>, BETWEEN, and IN. For example, the following predicates can be matched to an Index Seek operation if there is an index on the specified column, or a multi-column index with that column as a leading index key:

- ProductID = 771

- UnitPrice < 3.975

- LastName = 'Allen'

- LastName LIKE 'Brown%'

As an example, look at the next query, which uses an Index Seek operator and produces the plan in Figure 4-1.

```
SELECT ProductID, SalesOrderID, SalesOrderDetailID
FROM Sales.SalesOrderDetail
WHERE ProductID = 771
```

Listing 4-1.

Figure 4-1: Plan with Index Seek.

Index Seek (NonClustered)	
Scan a particular range of rows from a nonclustered index.	
Physical Operation	Index Seek
Logical Operation	Index Seek
Actual Number of Rows	241
Estimated I/O Cost	0.003125
Estimated CPU Cost	0.0004221
Estimated Number of Executions	1
Number of Executions	1
Estimated Operator Cost	0.0035471 (100%)
Estimated Subtree Cost	0.0035471
Estimated Number of Rows	241
Estimated Row Size	19 B
Actual Rebinds	0
Actual Rewinds	0
Ordered	True
Node ID	0

Object
[AdventureWorks].[Sales].[SalesOrderDetail].
[IX_SalesOrderDetail_ProductID]
Output List
[AdventureWorks].[Sales].[SalesOrderDetail].SalesOrderID,
[AdventureWorks].[Sales].
[SalesOrderDetail].SalesOrderDetailID, [AdventureWorks].
[Sales].[SalesOrderDetail].ProductID
Seek Predicates
Seek Keys[1]: Prefix: [AdventureWorks].[Sales].
[SalesOrderDetail].ProductID = Scalar Operator
(CONVERT_IMPLICIT(int,[@1],0))

Figure 4-2: Index Seek operator properties.

The `SalesOrderDetail` table has a multi-column index with `ProductID` as the leading column. The Index Seek operator properties, which you can see in Figure 4-2, include the following Seek predicate on the `ProductID` column, which shows that SQL Server was effectively able to use the index to seek on this column.

```
Seek Keys[1]: Prefix: [AdventureWorks].[Sales]. [SalesOrderDetail].ProductID =
Scalar Operator (CONVERT_IMPLICIT(int,[@1],0))
```
Listing 4-2.

An index cannot be used to seek on some complex expressions, expressions using functions, or strings with a leading wildcard character, as in the following predicates:

- ABS(ProductID) = 771

- UnitPrice + 1 < 3.975

- LastName LIKE '%Allen'

- UPPER(LastName) = 'Allen'

Compare the following query to the previous example; by adding an **ABS** function to the predicate, SQL Server is no longer able to use an Index Seek operator and chooses, instead, to do an Index Scan as shown on the plan in Figure 4-3.

```
SELECT ProductID, SalesOrderID, SalesOrderDetailID
FROM Sales.SalesOrderDetail
WHERE ABS(ProductID) = 771
```

Listing 4-3.

Figure 4-3: Plan with an Index Scan.

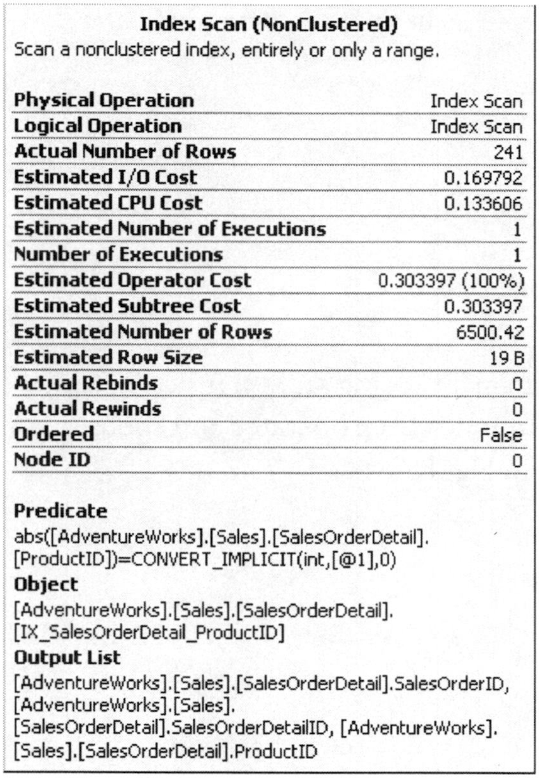

Index Scan (NonClustered)	
Scan a nonclustered index, entirely or only a range.	
Physical Operation	Index Scan
Logical Operation	Index Scan
Actual Number of Rows	241
Estimated I/O Cost	0.169792
Estimated CPU Cost	0.133606
Estimated Number of Executions	1
Number of Executions	1
Estimated Operator Cost	0.303397 (100%)
Estimated Subtree Cost	0.303397
Estimated Number of Rows	6500.42
Estimated Row Size	19 B
Actual Rebinds	0
Actual Rewinds	0
Ordered	False
Node ID	0

Predicate
abs([AdventureWorks].[Sales].[SalesOrderDetail].
[ProductID])=CONVERT_IMPLICIT(int,[@1],0)
Object
[AdventureWorks].[Sales].[SalesOrderDetail].
[IX_SalesOrderDetail_ProductID]
Output List
[AdventureWorks].[Sales].[SalesOrderDetail].SalesOrderID,
[AdventureWorks].[Sales].
[SalesOrderDetail].SalesOrderDetailID, [AdventureWorks].
[Sales].[SalesOrderDetail].ProductID

Figure 4-4: Index Scan operator properties.

Note that, in Figure 4-4, the following predicate is, however, still evaluated on the Index Scan operator.

```
abs([AdventureWorks].[Sales].[SalesOrderDetail].
[ProductID]) =CONVERT_IMPLICIT(int,[@1],0)
```

Listing 4-4.

In the case of a multi-column index, SQL Server can only use the index to seek on the second column if there is an equality predicate on the first column. So SQL Server can use

128

a multi-column index to seek on both columns in the following cases, supposing that a multi-column index exists on both columns in the order presented:

- ProductID = 771 AND SalesOrderID > 34000

- LastName = 'Smith' AND FirstName = 'Ian'

That being said, if there is no equality predicate on the first column, or if the predicate can not be evaluated on the second column, as is the case in a complex expression, then SQL Server may still only be able to use a multi-column index to seek on just the first column, as in the following examples:

- ProductID = 771 AND ABS(SalesOrderID) = 34000

- ProductID < 771 AND SalesOrderID = 34000

- LastName > 'Smith' AND FirstName = 'Ian'

However, SQL Server is *not* able to use a multi-column index for an Index Seek in the following examples, as it is not even able to search on the first column:

- ABS(ProductID) = 771 AND SalesOrderID = 34000

- LastName LIKE '%Smith' AND FirstName = 'Ian'

Finally, take a look at the following query, and the Index Seek operator properties in Figure 4-5.

```
SELECT ProductID, SalesOrderID, SalesOrderDetailID
FROM Sales.SalesOrderDetail
WHERE ProductID = 771 AND ABS(SalesOrderID) = 45233
```

Listing 4-5.

```
Index Seek (NonClustered)
Scan a particular range of rows from a nonclustered index.

Physical Operation                          Index Seek
Logical Operation                           Index Seek
Actual Number of Rows                                0
Estimated I/O Cost                           0.003125
Estimated CPU Cost                          0.0004221
Number of Executions                                 1
Estimated Number of Executions                       1
Estimated Operator Cost          0.0035471 (100%)
Estimated Subtree Cost                      0.0035471
Estimated Number of Rows                      12.9133
Estimated Row Size                                19 B
Actual Rebinds                                       0
Actual Rewinds                                       0
Ordered                                           True
Node ID                                              0

Predicate
abs([AdventureWorks].[Sales].[SalesOrderDetail].
[SalesOrderID])=[@2]
Object
[AdventureWorks].[Sales].[SalesOrderDetail].
[IX_SalesOrderDetail_ProductID]
Output List
[AdventureWorks].[Sales].[SalesOrderDetail].SalesOrderID,
[AdventureWorks].[Sales].
[SalesOrderDetail].SalesOrderDetailID, [AdventureWorks].
[Sales].[SalesOrderDetail].ProductID
Seek Predicates
Seek Keys[1]: Prefix: [AdventureWorks].[Sales].
[SalesOrderDetail].ProductID = Scalar Operator
(CONVERT_IMPLICIT(int,[@1],0))
```

Figure 4-5:   Index Seek operator properties.

The seek predicate is using only the `ProductID` column as shown here:

```
Seek Keys[1]: Prefix: [AdventureWorks].[Sales].
[SalesOrderDetail].ProductID = Scalar Operator (CONVERT_IMPLICIT(int,[@1],0)
```

Listing 4-6.

An additional predicate on the `SalesOrderID` column is evaluated like any other scan predicate, as listed in:

```
abs([AdventureWorks].[Sales].[SalesOrderDetail]. [SalesOrderID])=[@2]
```

Listing 4-7.

So, in summary this shows that, as we expected, SQL Server was able to perform a seek operation on the `ProductID` column but, because of the use of the ABS function, was not able to do the same for `SalesOrderID`. The index was used to navigate directly to find the rows that satisfy the first predicate, but then had to continue scanning to validate the second predicate.

The Database Engine Tuning Advisor

Currently, all major commercial database vendors include a physical database design tool to help with the creation of indexes. However, when these tools were first developed, there were just two main architectural approaches considered for how the tools should recommend indexes. The first approach was to build a stand-alone tool with its own cost model and design rules. The second approach was to build a tool that could use the Query Optimizer cost model.

A problem with building a stand-alone tool is the requirement for duplicating the cost module. On top of that, having a tool with its own cost model, even if it's better than the optimizer's cost model, may not be a good idea because the optimizer still chooses its plan based on *its own* model.

The second approach, using the Query Optimizer to help on physical database design, was proposed in the database research community as far as back as 1988. Since it's the optimizer which chooses the indexes for an execution plan, it makes sense to use the optimizer itself to help find which missing indexes would benefit existing queries. In this scenario, the physical design tool would use the optimizer to evaluate the cost of queries given a set of candidate indexes. An additional benefit of this approach is that, as the optimizer cost model evolves, any tool using its cost model can automatically benefit from it.

SQL Server was the first commercial database product to include a physical design tool, in the shape of the Index Tuning Wizard which shipped with SQL Server 7.0, and which was later replaced by the Database Engine Tuning Advisor (DTA) in SQL Server 2005. Both tools use the Query Optimizer cost model approach and were created as part of the AutoAdmin project at Microsoft, the goal of which was to reduce the total cost of ownership (TCO) of databases by making them self-tuning and self-managing. In addition to indexes, the DTA can help with the creation of indexed views and table partitioning.

However, creating real indexes in a DTA tuning session is not feasible; its overhead could impact operational queries and degrade the performance of your database. So how does the DTA estimate the cost of using an index that does not yet exist? Actually, even during a regular query optimization, the Query Optimizer does not use indexes to estimate the cost of a query. The decision on whether to use an index or not relies only on some metadata and the statistical information regarding the columns of the index. Index data itself is not needed during query optimization but will, of course, be required during query execution if the index is chosen.

So, to avoid creating real indexes during a DTA session, SQL Server uses a special kind of indexes called hypothetical indexes, which were also used by the Index Tuning Wizard. As the name implies, hypothetical indexes are not real indexes; they only contain statistics and can be created with the undocumented WITH STATISTICS_ONLY option of the CREATE INDEX statement. You may not be able to see these indexes during a DTA session because they are dropped automatically when they are no longer needed. However, you could see the CREATE INDEX WITH STATISTICS_ONLY and DROP INDEX statements if you run a SQL Server Profiler session to see what the DTA is doing.

Let's take a quick tour to some of these concepts. To get started, create a new table on the **AdventureWorks** database:

```
SELECT *
INTO dbo.SalesOrderDetail
FROM Sales.SalesOrderDetail
```

Listing 4-8.

Copy the following query and save it to a file:

```
SELECT * FROM dbo.SalesOrderDetail
WHERE ProductID = 897
```

Listing 4-9.

Open a new DTA session, and you can optionally run a SQL Server Profiler session if you want to inspect what the DTA is doing. On the **Workload File** option, select the file containing the SQL statement that you just created with Listing 4-9, and specify **AdventureWorks** as both the database to tune and the database for workload analysis. Click the **Start Analysis** button and, when the DTA analysis finishes, run this query to inspect the contents of the **msdb..DTA_reports_query** table:

```
SELECT * FROM msdb..DTA_reports_query
```

Listing 4-10.

Running that query shows the following output, (edited for space):

```
StatementString                                CurrentCost  RecommendedCost
---------------------------------------------  -----------  ---------------
SELECT * FROM dbo.SalesOrderDetail WHERE... 1.2434          0.00328799
```

Listing 4-11.

Notice that the query returns information like the query that was tuned, as well as the current and recommended cost. The current cost, 1.2434, is easy to obtain by directly requesting an estimated execution plan for the query as shown in Figure 4-6.

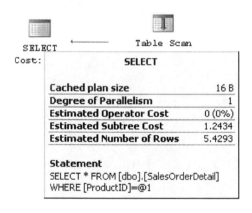

Figure 4-6: Plan showing total cost.

Since the DTA analysis was completed, the required hypothetical indexes were already dropped. To now obtain the indexes recommended by the DTA, click on the **Recommendations** tab and look at the **Index Recommendations** section, where you can find the code to create any recommended index by then clicking on the **Definition** column. In our example, it will show the code in Listing 4-12.

```
CREATE CLUSTERED INDEX [_dta_index_SalesOrderDetail_c_5_1915153868__K5]
ON [dbo].[SalesOrderDetail]
(
    [ProductID] ASC
)WITH (SORT_IN_TEMPDB = OFF, IGNORE_DUP_KEY = OFF, DROP_EXISTING = OFF,
ONLINE = OFF) ON [PRIMARY]
```
Listing 4-12.

In the next statement, and for demonstration purposes only, I will go ahead and create the index recommended by the DTA but, instead of a regular index, I will create it as a hypothetical index by adding the WITH STATISTICS_ONLY clause.

```
CREATE CLUSTERED INDEX cix_ProductID ON dbo.SalesOrderDetail(ProductID)
WITH STATISTICS_ONLY
```
Listing 4-13.

You can validate that a hypothetical index was created by running the next query:

```
SELECT * FROM sys.indexes
WHERE object_id = object_id('dbo.SalesOrderDetail')
AND name = 'cix_ProductID'
```
Listing 4-14.

The output is shown next below; note that the is_hypothetical field shows that this is, in fact, just a hypothetical index.

```
object_id   name           index_id type  type_desc is_hypothetical
----------  -------------  -------- ----- --------- ----------------
1915153868 cix_ProductID 3          1     CLUSTERED 1
```
Listing 4-15.

Remove the hypothetical index by running this statement:

```
DROP INDEX dbo.SalesOrderDetail.cix_ProductID
```

Listing 4-16.

Finally, implement the DTA recommendation, this time as a regular clustered index:

```
CREATE CLUSTERED INDEX cix_ProductID ON dbo.SalesOrderDetail(ProductID)
```

Listing 4-17.

After implementing the recommendation and running the query again, the clustered index is in fact now being used by the Query Optimizer. This time, the plan shows a Clustered Index Seek operator and an estimated cost of 0.0033652, which is very close to the recommended cost listed previously when querying the msdb..DTA_reports_ query table.

Finally, drop the table you just created by running the following statement:

```
DROP TABLE dbo.SalesOrderDetail
```

Listing 4-18.

The Missing Indexes Feature

SQL Server does provide a second approach that can help you to find useful indexes for your existing queries. Although not as powerful as the DTA, this option, called the Missing Indexes feature, does not require the database administrator to decide when tuning is needed, to explicitly identify what workload represents the load to tune, or to run any tool. This is a lightweight feature which is always on and, like the DTA, was also introduced with SQL Server 2005. Let's take a look at what it does.

During optimization, the Query Optimizer defines what the best indexes for a query are and, if these indexes don't exist, it will make this index information available in the XML plan for a particular plan (as well as the graphical plan, as of SQL Server Management Studio 2008). Alternatively, it will aggregate this information for queries optimized since the instance was started, and make it all available on the `sys.dm_db_missing_index` DMVs. Note that, just by displaying this information, the Query Optimizer is not only warning you that it might not be selecting an efficient plan; it is also showing you which indexes *may* help to improve the performance of your query. In addition, database administrators and developers should be aware of the limitations of this feature, as described on the Books Online entry, *Limitations of the Missing Indexes Feature*.

So, with all that in mind, let's take a quick look to see how this feature works. Create the `dbo.SalesOrderDetail` table on the `AdventureWorks` database by running the following statement:

```
SELECT *
INTO dbo.SalesOrderDetail
FROM sales.SalesOrderDetail
```

Listing 4-19.

Run this query and request a graphical or XML execution plan:

```
SELECT * FROM dbo.SalesOrderDetail
WHERE SalesOrderID = 43670 AND SalesOrderDetailID > 112
```
Listing 4-20.

This query could benefit from an index on the `SalesOrderID` and `SalesOrder-DetailID` columns, but no missing indexes information is shown this time. One limitation of the Missing Indexes feature which this example has revealed is that it does not work with a trivial plan optimization. You can verify that this is a trivial plan by looking at the graphical plan properties, shown as Optimization Level `TRIVIAL`, or by looking at the XML plan, where the `StatementOptmLevel` is shown as `TRIVIAL`.

You can avoid the trivial plan optimization in several ways, as I'll explain in *Chapter 5, The Optimization Process* (for now, you'll just have to take it on faith). In our case, we're just going to create a non-related index by running the following statement:

```
CREATE INDEX IX_ProductID ON dbo.SalesOrderDetail(ProductID)
```
Listing 4-21.

What is significant about this is that, although the index created will not be used by our previous query, the query no longer qualifies for a trivial plan. Run the query again, and this time the XML plan will contain the following entry:

```
<MissingIndexes>
  <MissingIndexGroup Impact="99.7137">
    <MissingIndex Database="[AdventureWorks]" Schema="[dbo]"
Table="[SalesOrderDetail]">
      <ColumnGroup Usage="EQUALITY">
        <Column Name="[SalesOrderID]" ColumnId="1" />
      </ColumnGroup>
```

```
        <ColumnGroup Usage="INEQUALITY">
        <Column Name="[SalesOrderDetailID]" ColumnId="2"/>
        </ColumnGroup>
      </MissingIndex>
    </MissingIndexGroup>
  </MissingIndexes>
```

Listing 4-22.

The `MissingIndexes` entry in the XML plan can show up to three groups: **equality**, **inequality**, and **included**; and the first two are shown in this example using the `ColumnGroup` attribute. The information contained in these groups can be used to create the missing index; the key of the index can be built by using the equality columns, followed by the inequality columns, and the included columns can be added using the `INCLUDE` clause of the `CREATE INDEX` statement. SQL Server 2008 Management Studio can build the `CREATE INDEX` statement for you and, in fact, if you look at the graphical plan, you can see a Missing Index warning at the top, including a `CREATE INDEX` command, as shown in Figure 4-7:

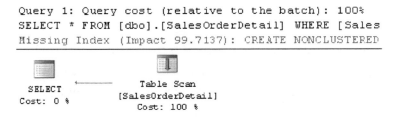

```
Query 1: Query cost (relative to the batch): 100%
SELECT * FROM [dbo].[SalesOrderDetail] WHERE [Sales
Missing Index (Impact 99.7137): CREATE NONCLUSTERED
```

```
   SELECT          Table Scan
   Cost: 0 %     [SalesOrderDetail]
                   Cost: 100 %
```

Figure 4-7:   Plan with a Missing Index warning.

Notice the impact value of 99.7137 – **Impact** is a number between 0 and 100 which gives you an estimate of the average percentage benefit that the query could obtain if the proposed index were available.

You can right-click on the graphical plan and select **Missing Index Details** to see the `CREATE INDEX` command that can be used to create this desired index, as shown in Listing 4-23.

```
/*
Missing Index Details from SQLQuery1.sql — The Query Processor estimates that
implementing the following index could improve the query cost by 99.7137%.
*/
/*
USE [AdventureWorks]
GO
CREATE NONCLUSTERED INDEX [<Name of Missing Index, sysname,>]
ON [dbo].[SalesOrderDetail] ([SalesOrderID], [SalesOrderDetailID])
GO
*/
```

Listing 4-23.

Create the recommended index, after you provide a name for it, by running the
following statement:

```
CREATE NONCLUSTERED INDEX IX_SalesOrderID_SalesOrderDetailID
ON [dbo].[SalesOrderDetail]([SalesOrderID], [SalesOrderDetailID])
```

Listing 4-24.

If you run the query in Listing 4-20 again and look at the execution plan, this time you'll
see an Index Seek operator using the index you've just created, and both the Missing
Index warning and the `MissingIndex` element of the XML plan are gone, as shown in
Figure 4-8.

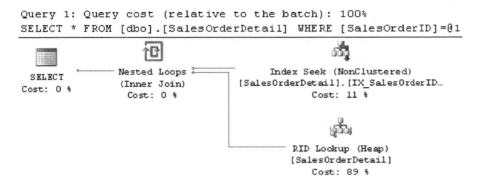

Figure 4-8: Plan without the Missing Index warning.

Finally, remove the **dbo.SalesOrderDetail** table you've just created by running the following statement:

```
DROP TABLE dbo.SalesOrderDetail
```

Listing 4-25.

Unused Indexes

I'll end this chapter on indexes by introducing the functionality of the **sys.dm_db_index_usage_stats** DMV, which you can use to learn about the operations performed by your indexes, and which is especially helpful in discovering indexes that are not used by any query, or are only minimally used. As we've already discussed, indexes that are not being used will provide no benefit to your databases, but *will* use valuable disk space, slow your update operations, and should be considered for removal.

The **sys.dm_db_index_usage_stats** DMV stores the number of seek, scan, lookup, and update operations performed by both user and system queries, including the last time each type of operation was performed. Keep in mind that this DMV, in addition to non-clustered indexes, will also include heaps, listed as `index_id` equal to 0, and clustered indexes, listed as `index_id` equal to 1. For the purposes of this section, you may want to just focus on non-clustered indexes, which include `index_id` values 2 or greater. Since heaps and clustered indexes contain the table's data, they may not even be candidates for removal in the first place.

By inspecting the `user_seeks`, `user_scans`, and `user_lookup` values of your non-clustered indexes you can see how your indexes are being used, and you can inspect the `user_updates` values to see the amount of updates performed on the index. All of this information will help to give you a sense as to how useful an index actually is. Bear in mind that all I'll be demonstrating is how to call up information from this DMV, and what sort of situations will trigger different updates to the information it returns. How you react to the information it returns is a task I leave to you.

As an example, run the following code to create a new table with a non-clustered index:

```
SELECT * INTO dbo.SalesOrderDetail
FROM Sales.SalesOrderDetail
CREATE NONCLUSTERED INDEX IX_ProductID ON dbo.SalesOrderDetail(ProductID)
```

Listing 4-26.

If you want to keep track of the values for this example follow these steps carefully, as every query execution may change the index usage statistics. When you run the following query, it will initially contain only one record, which was created because of table access performed when the index on Listing 4-26 was created.

```
SELECT DB_NAME(database_id) as database_name,
OBJECT_NAME(s.object_id) as object_name, i.name, s.*
FROM sys.dm_db_index_usage_stats s join sys.indexes i
ON s.object_id = i.object_id AND s.index_id = i.index_id
and s.object_id = object_id('dbo.SalesOrderDetail')
```

Listing 4-27.

However, the values that we will be inspecting in this exercise, `user_seeks`, `user_scans`, `user_lookups`, and `user_updates` are all set to 0.

Now run the following query, let's say, three times:

```
SELECT * FROM dbo.SalesOrderDetail
```
Listing 4-28.

This query is using a Table Scan operator, so, if you rerun the code in Listing 4-27, the DMV will show the value 3 on the `user_scans` column. Note that the column `index_id` is 0, denoting a heap, and the name of the table is also listed (as a heap is just a table with no clustered index).

Run the next query, which uses an Index Seek, twice. After the query is executed, a new record will be added for the non-clustered index, and the `user_seeks` counter will show a value of 2.

```
SELECT ProductID FROM dbo.SalesOrderDetail
WHERE ProductID = 773
```
Listing 4-29.

Now, run the following query four times, and it will use both Index Seek and RID Lookup operators. Since the `user_seeks` for the non-clustered index had a value of 2, it will be updated to 6, and the `user_lookups` value for the heap will be updated to 4.

```
SELECT * FROM dbo.SalesOrderDetail
WHERE ProductID = 773
```
Listing 4-30.

Finally, run the following query once:

```
UPDATE dbo.SalesOrderDetail
SET ProductID = 666
WHERE ProductID = 927
```

Listing 4-31.

Note that the **UPDATE** statement is doing an Index Seek and a Table Update, so user_seek will be updated for the index, and user_updates will be updated once for both the non-clustered index and the heap. This is the final output of the query in Listing 4-27 (edited for space):

```
name           index_id user_seeks user_scans user_lookups user_updates
-------------  -------- ---------- ---------- ------------ ------------
NULL           0        0          3          4            1
IX_ProductID   2        7          0          0            1
```

Listing 4-32.

Finally, drop the table you just created:

```
DROP TABLE dbo.SalesOrderDetail
```

Listing 4-33.

Summary

This chapter explained how you can define the key of your indexes so that they are likely to be considered for seek operations, which can improve the performance of your queries by finding records more quickly. Predicates were analyzed in the contexts of both single and multi-column indexes, and we also covered how to verify an execution plan to validate that indexes were selected and properly used by SQL Server.

The Database Engine Tuning Advisor and the Missing Indexes feature, both introduced with SQL Server 2005, were presented to show how the Query Optimizer itself can be used to provide index tuning recommendations.

Finally, the `sys.dm_db_index_usage_stats` DMV was introduced, together with its ability to provide valuable information regarding your non-clustered indexes usage. While we didn't have time to discuss all the practicalities of using this DMV, we covered enough for you to be able to easily find non-clustered indexes that are not being used by your SQL Server instance.

Chapter 5: The Optimization Process

In this chapter, I'll go into the internals of the Query Optimizer and introduce the steps that it performs in the background, and which we don't see. This covers everything, from the time a query is submitted to SQL Server until an execution plan is generated and is ready to be executed, and includes steps like parsing, binding, simplification, trivial plan optimization and full optimization. Important components which are part of the Query Optimizer architecture, such as transformation rules and the memo structure, are also introduced.

The purpose of the Query Optimizer, as we're all aware, is to provide an optimum execution plan and, in order to do so, it generates possible alternative execution plans through the use of transformation rules. These alternative plans are stored for the duration of the optimization process in a structure called the memo. Given that finding the optimum plan for some queries would take an unacceptably long optimization time, some heuristics are used to limit the number of alternative plans considered, instead of using the entire search space – remember that the goal is to find *a good enough plan as quickly as possible*. Heuristics help the Query Optimizer to cope with the combinatorial explosion which occurs in the search space as queries get progressively more complex. However, the use of transformation rules and heuristics does not necessarily reduce the cost of the available alternatives, so each candidate plan is also costed, and the best alternative is chosen based on those costs.

Overview

The query optimization and execution process were introduced in *Chapter 1, Introduction to Query Optimization*, and will be explained in more detail throughout the rest of this chapter. However, before we get started, I'll very briefly describe the inner workings of the query optimization process, which extends both before and after the Query Optimizer itself. So, if I mention terminology or concepts you've not seen before, don't panic – I'll go into much more detail and explain everything as we go through the chapter.

Parsing and binding are the first operations performed when a query is submitted to a SQL Server instance. They produce a tree representation of the query, which is then sent to the Query Optimizer to perform the optimization process. At the beginning of this optimization process, this logical tree will be simplified, and the Query Optimizer will check if the query qualifies for a trivial plan. If it does, then a trivial execution plan is returned and the optimization process immediately ends. The parsing, binding, simplification and trivial plan processes do not depend on the contents of the database (such as the statistics and the data itself), but only on the database schema and query definition. These processes also don't use statistics, cost estimation or cost-based decisions, all of which are only employed during the full optimization process.

If the query does not qualify for a trivial plan, then the Query Optimizer will run the full optimization process, which is executed in up to three stages, and a plan may be produced at the end of any of these stages. In addition, to consider all of the information gathered in the previous phases, like the query definition and database schema, the full optimization process will also use statistics and cost estimation, and will select the best execution plan (within the available time) based solely on that plan's cost.

Peeking at the Query Optimizer

In this section I will show you two DMVs which you can use to gain additional insight into the work being performed by the Query Optimizer. The first one, **sys.dm_exec_query_optimizer_info**, which is only partially documented, provides information regarding the optimizations performed on the SQL Server instance. The second one, **sys.dm_exec_query_transformation_stats**, which is also undocumented, provides information regarding how the Query Optimizer is using the defined transformation rules. Although both DMVs contain cumulative statistics, recorded since the given SQL Server instance was started, they can also be used to get optimization information for a specific query or workload, as we'll see in a moment.

Let us look at `sys.dm_exec_query_optimizer_info` first; as mentioned, you can use this DMV to obtain statistics regarding the operation of the Query Optimizer, such as how queries have been optimized, and how many of them have been optimized since the instance started. This DMV returns three columns:

- **Counter** – the name of the optimizer event
- **Occurrence** – the number of occurrences of the optimization event for this counter
- **Value** – the average value per event occurrence.

38 counters were defined for SQL Server 2005, and a new one, called `merge stmt`, was added in SQL Server 2008, giving a total of 39.

To view the statistics for all the Query Optimizer events since the SQL Server instance was started, we can just run:

```
SELECT * FROM sys.dm_exec_query_optimizer_info
```

Listing 5-1.

Table 5-1 shows some example output from one of my SQL Server instances. It shows that there have been 691,473 optimizations since the instance was started, that the average elapsed time for each optimization was 0.0078 seconds, and that the average estimated cost of each optimization, in internal cost units, was about 1.398. This particular example shows optimizations of inexpensive queries, typical of an OLTP system.

Counter	Occurrence	Value
optimizations	691473	1
elapsed time	691465	0.007806012
final cost	691465	1.398120739
trivial plan	29476	1
tasks	661989	332.5988816
no plan	0	NULL
search 0	26724	1
search 0 time	31420	0.01646922
search 0 tasks	31420	1198.811617

Table 5-1.

The query shown in Listing 5-2 displays the percentage of optimizations in the system that include hints. This information could be useful to show how extensive the use of hints in your application is, which, in turn, can show that your code may be less flexible than anticipated, and may require additional maintenance. Hints are explained in detail in chapter 7.

```
SELECT    ( SELECT  occurrence
            FROM    sys.dm_exec_query_optimizer_info
            WHERE   counter = 'hints'
          ) * 100.0 / ( SELECT  occurrence
                        FROM
                            sys.dm_exec_query_optimizer_info
                        WHERE   counter = 'optimizations'
                      )
```

Listing 5-2.

Although the `sys.dm_exec_query_optimizer_info` DMV was completely documented in the original version of SQL Server 2005 Books Online, more recent versions omit descriptions of nearly half (18 out of 39) of the counters, and instead label them as "Internal only."

Therefore, in Table 5-2, I am including the current Books Online documentation plus descriptions of the 18 undocumented counters, according to their original documentation, which is still valid for SQL Server 2008 R2. The additional descriptions are shown in italics.

Counter	Occurrence	Value
optimizations	Total number of optimizations.	Not applicable.
elapsed time	Total number of optimizations.	Average elapsed time per optimization of an individual statement (query), in seconds.
final cost	Total number of optimizations.	Average estimated cost for an optimized plan, in internal cost units.
trivial plan	*Total number of trivial plans (used as final plan).*	*Not applicable.*
tasks	*Number of optimizations that applied tasks (exploration, implementation, property derivation).*	*Average number of tasks executed.*
no plan	*Number of optimizations for which no plan was found after a full optimization was run, and where no other errors were issued during query compilation.*	*Not applicable.*

search 0	*Total number of final plans found in search 0 phase.*	*Not applicable.*
search 0 time	*Number of optimizations that entered search 0.*	*Average time spent in search 0, in seconds.*
search 0 tasks	*Number of optimizations that entered search 0.*	*Average number of tasks run in search 0.*
search 1	*Total number of final plans found in search 1 phase.*	*Not applicable.*
search 1 time	*Number of optimizations that entered search 1.*	*Average time spent in search 1, in seconds.*
search 1 tasks	*Number of optimizations that entered search 1.*	*Average number of tasks run in search 1.*
search 2	*Total number of final plans found in search 2 phase.*	*Not applicable.*
search 2 time	Total number of final plans found in search 2 phase.	Average time spent in search 2.
search 2 tasks	*Number of optimizations that entered search 2.*	*Average number of tasks run in search 2.*
gain stage 0 to stage 1	*Number of times search 1 was run after search 0.*	*Average gain from stage 0 to stage 1 as (MinimumPlanCost(search 0) − MinimumPlanCost(search 1)) / MinimumPlanCost(search 0).*
gain stage 1 to stage 2	*Number of times search 2 was run after search 1.*	*Average gain from stage 1 to stage 2 as (MinimumPlanCost(search 1) − MinimumPlanCost(search 2)) / MinimumPlanCost(search 1).*

timeout	*Number of optimizations for which internal timeout occurred.*	*Not applicable.*
memory limit exceeded	*Number of optimizations for which an internal memory limit was exceeded.*	*Not applicable.*
insert stmt	Number of optimizations that are for `INSERT` statements.	Not applicable.
delete stmt	Number of optimizations that are for `DELETE` statements.	Not applicable.
update stmt	Number of optimizations that are for `UPDATE` statements.	Not applicable.
merge stmt	Number of optimizations that are for `MERGE` statements.	Not applicable.
contains subquery	Number of optimizations for a query that contains at least one subquery.	Not applicable.
unnest failed	*Number of times where subquery unnesting could not remove the subquery.*	*Not applicable.*
tables	Total number of optimizations.	Average number of tables referenced per query optimized.

hints	Number of times some hint was specified. Hints counted include: JOIN, GROUP, UNION and FORCE ORDER query hints, FORCE PLAN set option, and join hints.	Not applicable.
order hint	Number of times a force order hint was specified.	Not applicable.
join hint	Number of times the join algorithm was forced by a join hint.	Not applicable.
view reference	Number of times a view has been referenced in a query.	Not applicable.
remote query	Number of optimizations where the query referenced at least one remote data source, such as a table with a four-part name or an OPENROWSET result.	Not applicable.
maximum DOP	Total number of optimizations.	Average effective MAXDOP value for an optimized plan. By default, effective MAXDOP is determined by the max degree of parallelism server configuration option, and may be overridden for a specific query by the value of the MAXDOP query hint.

maximum recursion level	Number of optimizations in which a MAXRECUR-SION level greater than 0 has been specified with the query hint.	Average MAXRECURSION level in optimizations where a maximum recursion level is specified with the query hint.
indexed views loaded	*Number of queries for which one or more indexed views were loaded for consideration for matching.*	*Average number of views loaded.*
indexed views matched	Number of optimizations where one or more indexed views have been matched.	Average number of views matched.
indexed views used	Number of optimizations where one or more indexed views are used in the output plan after being matched.	Average number of views used.
indexed views updated	Number of optimizations of a DML statement that produce a plan which maintains one or more indexed views.	Average number of views maintained.
dynamic cursor request	Number of optimizations in which a dynamic cursor request has been specified.	Not applicable.
fast-forward cursor request	Number of optimizations in which a fast-forward cursor request has been specified.	Not applicable.

Table 5-2:   Books Online documentation, with undocumented counters.

As mentioned previously, you can use this DMV in two different ways: you can use it to get information regarding the history of accumulated optimizations on the system since the instance was started or, rather more usefully, you can use it to get optimization information for a particular query or a workload.

In order to capture data on the latter, you need to take two snapshots of the DMV – one before optimizing your query, and another one after the query has been optimized – and manually find the difference between them. Unfortunately, there is no way to initialize the values of this DMV.

There are several issues to consider when capturing this information. Firstly, you need to eliminate the effects of system-generated queries, or queries executed by other users, which may be running at the same time as your sample query. Try to isolate the query or workload on your own instance, and make sure that the number of optimizations reported is the same as the number of optimizations you are requesting. If the former is greater, then the data probably includes some of those queries submitted by the system or other users. Of course, it's also possible that your own query against the `sys.dm_exec_query_optimizer_info` DMV may count as an optimization.

Secondly, you need to make sure that a query optimization is actually taking place. For example, if you run the same query more than once, then the Query Optimizer may simply use an existing plan from the plan cache. You can force an optimization by using the RECOMPILE hint, as shown later, or by clearing the plan cache. For instance, as of SQL Server 2008, the `DBCC FREEPROCCACHE` statement can be used to remove a specific plan, all the plans related to a specific resource pool, or the entire plan cache. But of course, you should never clear the plan cache of a production environment.

With all of this in mind, the script shown in Listing 5-3 will display the optimization information for a specific query, while avoiding all of the aforementioned issues. The script is based on an original idea by Lubor Kollar, and has a section to include the query which you want to get optimization information about.

```
- - optimize these queries now
- - so they do not skew the collected results
GO
SELECT *
INTO after_query_optimizer_info
FROM sys.dm_exec_query_optimizer_info
GO
SELECT *
INTO before_query_optimizer_info
FROM sys.dm_exec_query_optimizer_info
GO
DROP TABLE before_query_optimizer_info
DROP TABLE after_query_optimizer_info
GO
- - real execution starts
GO
SELECT *
INTO before_query_optimizer_info
FROM sys.dm_exec_query_optimizer_info
GO
- - insert your query here
SELECT *
FROM Person.Address
- - keep this to force a new optimization
OPTION (RECOMPILE)
GO
SELECT *
INTO after_query_optimizer_info
FROM sys.dm_exec_query_optimizer_info
GO
SELECT a.counter,
     (a.occurrence - b.occurrence) AS occurrence,
     (a.occurrence * a.value - b.occurrence *
    b.value) AS value
FROM before_query_optimizer_info b
    JOIN after_query_optimizer_info a
    ON b.counter = a.counter
WHERE b.occurrence <> a.occurrence
DROP TABLE before_query_optimizer_info
DROP TABLE after_query_optimizer_info
```

Listing 5-3.

Note that some queries are listed twice in the code. The purpose of this is to optimize them the first time that they are executed, so that their plan can be available in the plan cache for all the executions after that. In this way, we aim as far as possible to isolate the optimization information from the queries we are trying to analyze. Care must be taken that both queries are exactly the same, including case, comments, and so on, and separated in their own batch for the GO statements.

If you run this script against the **AdventureWorks** database, the output should look like what's shown in Table 5-3. Note that the times shown obviously may be different from the ones you get in your system, (for both this and other examples in this chapter). This table indicates, among other things, that there was one optimization, referencing one table, with a cost of 0.230042585.

Counter	Occurrence	Value
elapsed time	1	0
final cost	1	0.230042585
maximum DOP	1	0
optimizations	1	1
tables	1	1
trivial plan	1	1

Table 5-3.

Certainly, for this simple query, we could find the same information in some other places, such as in an execution plan. However, as I will show later in this chapter, this DMV can provide optimization information that is not available anywhere else.

The second DMV, **sys.dm_exec_query_transformation_stats**, provides information about the existing transformation rules and how they are being used by the Query

Optimizer. Similar to the **sys.dm_exec_query_optimizer_info** DMV, you can also use it to get optimization information for a particular query or workload by taking two snapshots of the DMV (before and after optimizing your query), and manually finding the difference between them.

To start looking at this DMV, run the following query:

```
SELECT * FROM sys.dm_exec_query_transformation_stats
```

Listing 5-4.

Table 5-4 contains a sample output in my test system using SQL Server 2008 R2, showing the first 10 records out of 377, and edited to fit the page.

Name	promise_avg	Promised	built_substitute	Succeeded
JNtoNL	49	2	0	0
LOJNtoNL	456.1428571	7	7	7
LSJNtoNL	0	0	0	0
LASJNtoNL	0	0	0	0
JNtoSM	454	2	2	2
FOJNtoSM	0	0	0	0
LOJNtoSM	454	7	7	0
ROJNtoSM	454	7	7	0
LSJNtoSM	0	0	0	0
RSJNtoSM	0	0	0	0

Table 5-4.

The `sys.dm_exec_query_transformation_stats` DMV returns the transformation rules currently defined in the system, of which there are 377 for the current release of SQL Server 2008 R2, and includes what is known as their **promise information**, which tells the Query Optimizer how useful a given transformation rule might be. The first field in the results output is the name of the rule; for example, the first three listed are JNtoNL (Join to Nested Loops Join), LOJNtoNL (Left Outer Join to Nested Loops Join), and JNtoSM (Join to Sort Merge Join), which is the academic name of the SQL Server Merge Join operator.

The same issues shown for the `sys.dm_exec_query_optimizer_info` DMV regarding collecting data also apply to the `sys.dm_exec_query_transformation_stats` DMV, so the following query can help you to isolate the optimization information for a specific query, while avoiding data from related queries as much as possible. The query is based on the **succeeded** column, which keeps track of the number of times a transformation rule was used and successfully produced a result.

```
- — optimize these queries now
- — so they do not skew the collected results
GO
SELECT *
INTO before_query_transformation_stats
FROM sys.dm_exec_query_transformation_stats
GO
SELECT *
INTO after_query_transformation_stats
FROM sys.dm_exec_query_transformation_stats
GO
DROP TABLE after_query_transformation_stats
DROP TABLE before_query_transformation_stats
- — real execution starts
GO
SELECT *
INTO before_query_transformation_stats
FROM sys.dm_exec_query_transformation_stats
GO
- — insert your query here
SELECT * FROM dbo.DatabaseLog
```

```
- - keep this to force a new optimization
OPTION (RECOMPILE)
GO
SELECT *
INTO after_query_transformation_stats
FROM sys.dm_exec_query_transformation_stats
GO
SELECT a.name, (a.promised - b.promised) as promised
FROM before_query_transformation_stats b
JOIN after_query_transformation_stats a
ON b.name = a.name
WHERE b.succeeded <> a.succeeded
DROP TABLE before_query_transformation_stats
DROP TABLE after_query_transformation_stats
```

Listing 5-5.

For example, testing with a very simple AdventureWorks query like the following, which is already included in the code in Listing 5-5 …

```
SELECT * FROM dbo.DatabaseLog
```

Listing 5-6.

… will show that the following transformation rules are being used.

name	promised
GetIdxToRng	1
GetToTrivialScan	1

Table 5-5.

We will be using these two DMVs in several sections later in this chapter, and you should, hopefully, come to see why they are very useful in providing additional insight into the work being performed by the Query Optimizer.

Parsing and Binding

Parsing and binding are the first operations that SQL Server executes when you submit a query to a database and, in the current version, they are performed by a component called the Algebrizer. **Parsing** first makes sure that the T-SQL query has a valid syntax, and then uses the query information to build a tree of relational operators. By that, I mean the parser translates the SQL query into an algebra tree representation of logical operators, which is called a parse tree.

Parsing only checks for valid T-SQL syntax, not for valid table or column names, which are verified in the next phase: **binding**.

Parsing is similar to the parse functionality available in Management Studio (by clicking the **Parse** button on the default toolbar) or the **SET PARSEONLY** statement. For example, the following query will successfully parse on the **AdventureWorks** database, even when the listed columns and table do not exist in said database.

```
SELECT lname, fname FROM authors
```

Listing 5-7.

However, if you incorrectly write the **SELECT** or **FROM** keywords, SQL Server will return an error message complaining about the incorrect syntax.

Once the parse tree has been constructed, the Algebrizer performs the binding operation, which is mostly concerned with name resolution. During this operation, the Algebrizer makes sure that all of the objects named in the query do actually exist, confirms that the requested operations between them are valid, and verifies that the objects are visible to the user running the query. It also associates every table and column name on the parse tree with their corresponding object in the system catalog. Name resolution for views includes the process of view substitution, where a view reference is expanded to include the view definition; for example, to directly include the tables used in the view. The output of the binding operation, which is called an algebrized tree, is then sent to the Query Optimizer for (as you'll have guessed) optimization.

Originally, this tree will be represented as a series of logical operations which are closely related to the original syntax of the query. These will include such logical operations as "get data from the Customer table," "get data from the Contact table," "perform an inner join," and so on. Different tree representations of the query will be used throughout the optimization process, and this logical tree will receive different names, until it is finally used to initialize the memo structure, as we'll discuss later.

For example, the following query will have a tree representation as shown in Figure 5-1.

```
SELECT c.CustomerID, COUNT(*)
FROM Sales.Customer c JOIN Sales.SalesOrderHeader o
ON c.CustomerID = o.CustomerID
WHERE c.TerritoryID = 4
GROUP BY c.CustomerID
```

Listing 5-8.

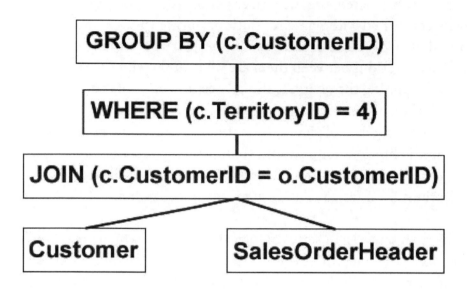

Figure 5-1:   Query tree representation.

Transformation Rules

The SQL Server Query Optimizer uses transformation rules to explore the search space; that is, to explore the set of possible execution plans for a specific query. Transformation rules are based on relational algebra, taking a relational operator tree and generating equivalent alternatives, in the form of equivalent relational operator trees. At the most fundamental level, a query consists of logical expressions, and applying these transformation rules will generate equivalent logical and physical alternatives, which are stored in memory, in a structure called the memo, for the entire duration of the optimization process. As already mentioned, and explained later in this chapter, the Query Optimizer uses three optimization stages, and different transformation rules are applied in each stage.

Each transformation rule has a pattern and a substitute. The pattern is the expression to be analyzed and matched, and the substitute is the equivalent expression that it is generated as an output. For example, for the commutativity rule, which is explained later, a transformation rule can be defined as: **Expr1 join Expr2 – > Expr2 join Expr1**.

SQL Server will match the pattern **Expr1 join Expr2**, like in **Individual join Customer**, and will produce the equivalent expression, **Customer join Individual**. The two expressions are equivalent because both return exactly the same results.

Initially, the query tree contains only logical expressions, and transformation rules are applied to these logical expressions to generate either logical or physical expressions. As an example, a logical expression can be the definition of a logical join, whereas a physical expression could be an actual join implementation, like a Merge Join or a Hash Join. Bear in mind that transformation rules cannot be applied to physical expressions.

The main types of transformation rules include simplification, exploration and implementation rules. Simplification rules produce simpler logical trees as their outputs, and are mostly used during the simplification phase, before the full optimization. Exploration rules, also called logical transformation rules, generate logical equivalent alternatives; and implementation rules, or physical transformation rules, are used to obtain physical alternatives. Both exploration and implementation rules are executed during the full optimization phase.

Examples of exploration rules include the commutativity and associativity rules, which are used in join optimization. Commutativity and associativity rules are defined as **A join B – > B join A** and **(A join B) join C – > A join (B join C)** respectively. The commutativity rule, **A join B – > B join A**, means that **A join B** is equivalent to **B join A**, and joining the tables A and B in any order will return the same results. Also note that applying the commutativity rule twice will generate the original expression again; that is, if you initially apply this transformation to obtain **B join A**, and then later apply the same transformation, you can obtain **A join B** again. However, the Query Optimizer can handle this problem in order to avoid duplicated expressions. In the same way, the associativity rule shows that **(A join B) join C** is equivalent to **A join (B join C)** as they also both produce the same results.

An example of an implementation rule would be selecting a physical algorithm for a logical join, such as a Merge Join or a Hash Join.

So the Query Optimizer is using sets of transformation rules to generate and examine possible alternative execution plans. However, it's important to remember that applying transformations does not necessarily reduce the cost of the generated alternatives, and the costing component still needs to estimate their costs. Although both logical and physical alternatives are kept in the memo structure, only the physical alternatives are costed. It's important, then, to bear in mind that, although these alternatives may be equivalent and return the same results, their physical implementations may have very different costs. The final selection, as is hopefully clear now, will be the best (or, if you like, the "cheapest") physical alternative stored in the memo.

For example, implementing **A join B** may have different costs depending on whether a Nested Loops Join or a Hash Join is selected. In addition, for the same physical join, implementing the **A join B** expression may have different performance from **B join A**. As explained in *Chapter 2, The Execution Engine*, the performance of a join is different depending on which table is chosen as the inner or outer table in a Nested Loops Join, or the build and the probe inputs in a Hash Join. If you want to find out why the Query Optimizer might not choose a specific join algorithm, you can use a hint to force a specific physical join and compare the cost of both the hinted and the original plans.

Those are the foundation principles of transformation rules and, as we saw briefly earlier in this chapter, according to the `sys.dm_exec_query_transformation_stats` DMV, SQL Server currently has 377 transformation rules, and more can be added in future versions of the product. Just as a point of reference, a quick look at the first Community Technology Preview (CTP) of the next version of SQL Server, code-named "Denali," already shows 382 transformation rules included in this DMV!

So, let's go back to the `sys.dm_exec_query_transformation_stats` DMV defined earlier and see a few examples of transformation rules used by the query processor. Include the following query into the code in Listing 5-5 to explore the transformation rules it uses:

```
SELECT c.CustomerID, COUNT(*)
FROM Sales.Customer c JOIN Sales.SalesOrderHeader o
ON c.CustomerID = o.CustomerID
GROUP BY c.CustomerID
```

Listing 5-9.

As shown in the following output, 17 transformation rules were exercised during the optimization process.

Name	Promised
AppIdxToApp	0
EnforceSort	23
GbAggBeforeJoin	4
GbAggToHS	8
GbAggToStrm	8
GenLGAgg	2
GetIdxToRng	0
GetToIdxScan	4
GetToScan	4
ImplRestrRemap	3
JNtoHS	6
JNtoIdxLookup	6
JNtoSM	6
JoinCommute	2

ProjectToComputeScalar	2
SelIdxToRng	6
SELonJN	1

Table 5-6.

Now, (as I will explain in more detail in *Chapter 7, Hints*) hints may disable some of these transformation rules for the duration of a query in order to obtain a specific desired behavior. As a way of experimenting with the effects of these rules, you can also use the undocumented statements DBCC RULEON and DBCC RULEOFF to enable or disable transformation rules, and thereby get additional insight into how the Query Optimizer works. However, before you do that, first be warned that, since these statements impact the entire optimization process performed by the Query Optimizer, they should be used only in a test system for experimentation purposes.

To demonstrate the effects of these statements, the query in Listing 5-9 shows the plan seen below in Figure 5-2.

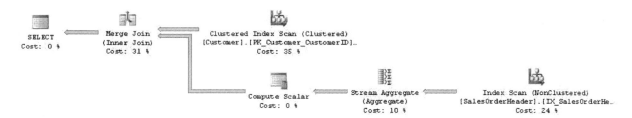

Figure 5-2: Original execution plan.

Here you can see, among other things, that SQL Server is pushing an aggregate below the join (a Stream Aggregate before the Merge Join). The Query Optimizer can push aggregations that significantly reduce cardinality estimation as early in the plan as possible. This is performed by the transformation rule **GbAggBeforeJoin** (or **Group By Aggregate Before Join**), which is included in the output of Table 5-6. This specific transformation rule is used only if certain requirements are met; for example, when the **GROUP BY** clause includes the joining columns, which is the case in our example. Run the following statement to temporarily disable the use of the **GbAggBeforeJoin** transformation rule for the current session:

```
DBCC RULEOFF('GbAggBeforeJoin')
```

Listing 5-10.

After disabling this transformation rule and running the query again, the plan, shown in Figure 5-3, will now show the aggregate after the join, which, according to the Query Optimizer, is a more expensive plan. You can verify this by looking at their estimated costs: 0.285331 and 0.312394, respectively. (These are not shown on the figures, but you can see them by hovering the mouse over the SELECT icon and examining the Estimated Subtree Cost value, as explained before.) Note that, for this exercise, an optimization may need to be forced to see the new plan, perhaps using the **OPTION (RECOMPILE)** hint or one of the methods which we've discussed to remove the plan from the cache, like DBCC FREEPROCCACHE.

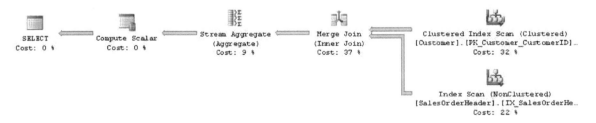

Figure 5-3:   Plan with **GbAggBeforeJoin** rule disabled.

In addition, there are a couple of additional undocumented statements to show which transformation rules are enabled and disabled, and these are DBCC SHOWONRULES and DBCC SHOWOFFRULES. By default, DBCC SHOWONRULES will list all the 377 transformation rules listed by the **sys.dm_exec_query_transformation_stats** DMV. To test it, try running the code in Listing 5-11.

169

```
DBCC TRACEON (3604)
DBCC SHOWONRULES
```

Listing 5-11.

We start this exercise with the DBCC TRACEON (3604) command, which enables trace flag 3604, and instructs SQL Server to send the results to the client, in this case, your Management Studio session. That means that, in this exercise, the output of the DBCC SHOWONRULES, and later DBCC SHOWOFFRULES, DBCC RULEON and DBCC RULEOFF statements will be conveniently available to us. An output similar to Listing 5-12 will be displayed in this first instance (only 12 rules out of 376 rules are shown here, to preserve space). The previously disabled rule will not be shown in this output.

```
DBCC execution completed. If DBCC printed error messages, contact your system administrator.
Rules that are on globally:
JNtoNL
LOJNtoNL
LSJNtoNL
LASJNtoNL
JNtoSM
FOJNtoSM
LOJNtoSM
ROJNtoSM
LSJNtoSM
RSJNtoSM
LASJNtoSM
RASJNtoSM
...
DBCC execution completed. If DBCC printed error messages, contact your system administrator.
```

Listing 5-12.

In the same way, the following code will show the rules that are disabled:

```
DBCC SHOWOFFRULES
```

Listing 5-13.

In our case, it will show that only one rule has been disabled:

```
DBCC execution completed. If DBCC printed error messages, contact your system administrator.
Rules that are off globally:
GbAggBeforeJoin
DBCC execution completed. If DBCC printed error messages, contact your system administrator.
```

Listing 5-14.

To continue with our example of the effects of the transformation rules, we can disable the use of a Merge Join by disabling the rule **JNtoSM** (Join to Sort Merge Join) by running the following code:

```
DBCC RULEOFF('JNtoSM')
```

Listing 5-15.

If you have followed the example, this time `DBCC RULEOFF` will show some output indicating that the rule is off for some specific `SPID`. Running the sample query again will give us this totally new plan, using both a Hash Join and a Hash Aggregate, as shown in Figure 5-4.

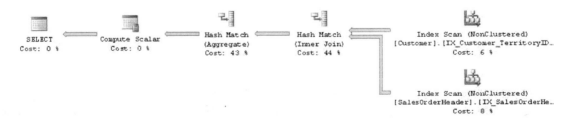

Figure 5-4: Plan with **JNtoSM** rule disabled.

In *Chapter 7, Hints*, you will learn how to obtain this same behavior in your queries using (unsurprisingly) hints.

Finally, before we finish, don't forget to re-enable the **GbAggBeforeJoin** and **JNtoSM** transformation rules by running the following commands …

```
DBCC RULEON('JNtoSM')
DBCC RULEON('GbAggBeforeJoin')
```

Listing 5-16.

… and verify that no transformation rules are still disabled, by running:

```
DBCC SHOWOFFRULES
```

Listing 5-17.

You may also want to clear your plan cache to make sure none of these experiment plans were left in memory, by once again running:

```
DBCC FREEPROCCACHE
```

Listing 5-18.

The Memo

The memo structure was originally defined in *The Volcano Optimizer Generator* by Goetz Graefe and William McKenna in 1993. As discussed in *Chapter 1, Introduction to Query Optimization*, the SQL Server Query Optimizer is based on the Cascades Framework, which was, in fact, a descendent of the Volcano optimizer.

The memo is a search data structure that is used to store the alternatives which are generated and analyzed by the Query Optimizer. These alternatives can be logical or physical operators, and are organized into groups of equivalent alternatives, such that each alternative in the same group produces the same results. Alternatives in the same group also share the same logical properties and, in the same way that operators can reference other operators on a relational tree, groups can also reference other groups in the memo structure.

A new memo structure is created for each optimization. The Query Optimizer first copies the original query tree's logical expressions into the memo structure, placing each operator from the query tree in its own group, and then triggers the entire optimization process. During this process, transformation rules are applied to generate all the alternatives, starting with these initial logical expressions.

As the transformation rules produce new alternatives, these are added to their equivalent groups. Transformation rules may also produce a new expression which is not equivalent to any existing group, and which causes a new group to be created. As I mentioned, each alternative in a group is a simple logical or physical expression, like a join or a scan, and a plan will be built using a combination of these alternatives. The number of these alternatives, and even groups, in a memo structure can be huge.

Although there is the possibility that different combinations of transformation rules may end up producing the same expressions, the memo structure is designed to avoid both the duplication of these alternatives and redundant optimizations. By doing this, it saves memory and is more efficient, as it does not have to search the same plan alternatives more than once.

Although both logical and physical alternatives are kept in the memo structure, only the physical alternatives are costed. Thus, at the end of the optimization process, the memo contains all of the alternatives considered by the Query Optimizer, but only one plan is selected, based on its cost.

Now, I will show a simplified example of how the memo structure is built for a simple query using listing 5-19.

```
SELECT FirstName, LastName, CustomerType
FROM Person.Contact AS C
    JOIN Sales.Individual AS I
        ON C.ContactID = I.ContactID
    JOIN Sales.Customer AS Cu
        ON I.CustomerID = Cu.CustomerID
```
Listing 5-19.

After a logical tree is created for this query, as explained before, each operator is placed in its own group, as shown in Table 5.7.

Group 6	Join 3 & 4
Group 5	
Group 4	Scan Customer
Group 3	Join 1 & 2
Group 2	Scan Individual
Group 1	Scan Contact

Table 5-7:   Initial memo structure.

Notice how both joins reference the other groups instead of the operators. We call Group 6 the root because it is the root operator of the initial plan, that is, it is the root node of the original query tree. I just left Group 5 blank so it is easier to introduce new groups and visualize the root group at the top. During optimization, several transformation rules will be executed, and they will create new alternatives. For example, if we apply either of the two following associativity rules ...

174

```
(Contact join Individual) join Customer — > Contact join(Individual join Customer)
```

Listing 5-20.

or

```
(1 join 2) join 4 — > 1 join(2 join 4)
```

Listing 5-21.

... we obtain two new operators that are not yet present in the memo structure. The first one is **Join 2 & 4**. Since we do not have an equivalent group for this new operator, we place it in a new group, Group 5 in this case. The second operator joins Group 1 and the new operator we just added to the memo structure. This new operator would be **Join 1 & 5**, and since **Join 1 & 5** is equivalent to **Join 3 & 4**, we place them in the same group, which is also the root group. These two changes are shown in Table 5-8.

Group 6	Join 3 & 4	Join 1 & 5
Group 5		Join 2 & 4
Group 4	Scan Customer	
Group 3	Join 1 & 2	
Group 2	Scan Individual	
Group 1	Scan Contact	

Table 5-8:   Memo structure after associativity rule has been applied.

175

We can show an example of the commutativity rule like this:

```
1 Join 5 — > 5 Join 1
```

Listing 5-22.

Since the new alternative is equivalent to the original operator, it is placed in the same group, as shown in Table 5-9, along with two other example operators which were added using the same commutativity rule.

Group 6	Join 3 & 4	Join 1 & 5	Join 5 & 1
Group 5		Join 2 & 4	Join 4 & 2
Group 4	Scan Customer		
Group 3	Join 1 & 2		Join 2 & 1
Group 2	Scan Individual		
Group 1	Scan Contact		

Table 5-9:   Memo structure after commutativity rule.

Given that this is a simplified example, and I imagine you've got the picture by now, I'll stop generating logical alternatives at this point. However, rest assured that the Query Optimizer has many other transformation rules in its arsenal with which to generate alternatives.

Towards the end of the process, after some implementation rules are applied, physical operators will be added to the memo structure. A few of them have been added to Table 5-10, and they include data access operators like Clustered Index Scan, and physical join operators like Nested Loops Join, together with Merge Join and Hash Join.

Group 6	Join 3 & 4	Join 1 & 5	Join 5 & 1	Nested Loops 5 & 1	**Hash Join 5 & 1**
Group 5		Join 2 & 4	Join 4 & 2	Nested Loops 2 & 4	**Merge Join 4 & 2**
Group 4	Scan Customer			**Clustered Index Scan**	
Group 3	Join 1 & 2		Join 2 & 1	Nested Loops 1 & 2	
Group 2	Scan Individual			**Clustered Index Scan**	
Group 1	Scan Contact			**Clustered Index Scan**	

Table 5-10:   Memo structure with physical operators.

After the cost is estimated for each physical operator, the Query Optimizer will look for the cheapest way to assemble a plan using the alternatives available. In our example, it would select the plan operators shaded in gray in Table 5-10. As a result, the execution plan selected by SQL Server is the plan shown in Figure 5-5, and you should notice that the Query Optimizer did not select the join order that was explicitly requested in the query text and shown in Group 1's tree representation. Instead, the Query Optimizer found a better join order with a lower cost.

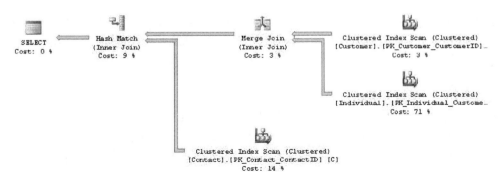

Figure 5-5:   Selected execution plan.

Optimization Phases

The Query Optimizer has several optimization phases designed to try to optimize queries as quickly and simply as possible, and to not use more expensive and sophisticated options unless absolutely necessary. These phases are called the **simplification**, **trivial plan optimization** and **full optimization** stages. In the same way, the full optimization phase itself consists of three stages simply called **search 0**, **search 1** and **search 2**.

Plans can be produced in any of these phases except for the simplification one, which I'll discuss in a moment. In this section, I'll use the `sys.dm_exec_query_optimizer_info` DMV, introduced earlier in this chapter, to show additional information about these optimization phases.

Simplification

Query rewrites or, more exactly, tree rewrites are performed on this stage to reduce the query tree into a simpler form in order to make the optimization process easier. Some of these simplifications include those below.

- Subqueries are converted into joins, but since a subquery does not always translate directly to an inner join, outer join and group by operations may be added as necessary.

- Redundant inner and outer joins may be removed. A typical example is the Foreign Key Join elimination which occurs when SQL Server can detect that some joins may not be needed, as foreign key constraints are available and only columns of the referencing table are requested. An example of Foreign Key Join elimination is shown later.

- Filters in WHERE clauses are pushed down in the query tree in order to enable early data filtering, and potentially better matching of indexes and computed columns later in the optimization process (this simplification is known as predicate pushdown).

- Contradictions are detected and removed. Since these parts of the query are not executed at all, SQL Server saves resources like I/O, locks, memory and CPU, making the query to be executed faster. For example, the Query Optimizer may know that no records can satisfy a predicate even before touching any page of data. A contradiction may be related to a check constraint, or may be related to the way the query is written. Both scenarios will be shown in an example later in this section.

The output of the simplification process is a simplified logical operator tree.

Let's see a couple of examples of the simplification process, starting with the Foreign Key Join elimination. The query we used on Listing 5-19 joins three tables and shows the execution plan seen in Figure 5-5. Let's see what happens if we comment out the `CustomerType` column, as shown in Listing 5-23.

```
SELECT FirstName, LastName — -, CustomerType
FROM Person.Contact AS C
    JOIN Sales.Individual AS I
        ON C.ContactID = I.ContactID
    JOIN Sales.Customer AS Cu
        ON I.CustomerID = Cu.CustomerID
```

Listing 5-23.

If you run the query again, this time only two tables are joined, and the `Customer` table has been removed, as can be seen in the execution plan in Figure 5-6.

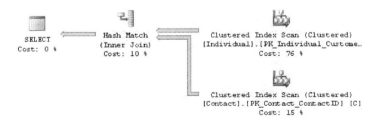

Figure 5-6:   Foreign Key Join elimination example.

There are two reasons for this change. First, since the `CustomerType` column is no longer required, there are no columns requested from the `Customer` table. However, it seems like the `Customer` table is still needed, as it is required as part of the equality operation on a join condition. That is, SQL Server needs to make sure that a `Customer` record exists for each related record on the `Individual` table.

Actually this validation is performed by the existing foreign key constraint, so the Query Optimizer realizes that there is no need to use the `Customer` table at all. As a test, temporarily disable the foreign key by running the following statement:

```
ALTER TABLE Sales.Individual NOCHECK CONSTRAINT FK_Individual_Customer_CustomerID
```

Listing 5-24.

Now run the Listing 5-23 query again. Without the foreign key constraint, SQL Server has no choice but to perform the join in order to make sure that the join condition is executed. As a result, it will use a plan joining all three tables, similar to the one shown previously in Figure 5-5. Finally, don't forget to re-enable the foreign key by running the statement in Listing 5-25.

```
ALTER TABLE Sales.Individual WITH CHECK CHECK CONSTRAINT
FK_Individual_Customer_CustomerID
```

Listing 5-25.

Now for an example of contradiction detection; first, I need a table with a check constraint and, handily, the `Employee` table has the following check constraint definition:

```
([VacationHours]>=(-40) AND [VacationHours]<=(240))
```

Listing 5-26.

This check constraint makes sure that the number of vacation hours is a number between −40 and 240, so if I request:

```
SELECT * FROM HumanResources.Employee
WHERE VacationHours > 80
```

Listing 5-27.

... SQL Server will use a Clustered Index Scan operator, as shown in Figure 5-7.

Figure 5-7: Plan without contradiction detection.

However, if I request all of the employees with more than 300 vacation hours then, because of this check constraint, the Query Optimizer must immediately know that no records qualify for predicate. Run the query in Listing 5-28.

```
SELECT * FROM HumanResources.Employee
WHERE VacationHours > 300
```

Listing 5-28.

As expected, the query will return no records, but this time it will show the execution plan shown in Figure 5-8.

Figure 5-8. Contradiction detection example.

Note that, this time, instead of a Clustered Index Scan, SQL Server is using a Constant Scan operator. Since there is no need to access the table at all, SQL Server saves resources like I/O, locks, memory and CPU, making the query to be executed faster.

Now, let's see what happens if I disable the check constraint:

```
ALTER TABLE HumanResources.Employee NOCHECK CONSTRAINT CK_Employee_VacationHours
```
Listing 5-29.

This time, running the Listing 5-28 query once again uses a Clustered Index Scan operator, as the Query Optimizer can no longer use the check constraint to guide its decisions. Don't forget to enable the constraint again by running the following statement:

```
ALTER TABLE HumanResources.Employee WITH CHECK CHECK CONSTRAINT CK_Employee_
VacationHours
```
Listing 5-30.

The second type of contradiction case is when the query itself explicitly contains a contradiction. Take a look at the query in Listing 5-31.

```
SELECT * FROM HumanResources.Employee
WHERE ManagerID > 10 AND ManagerID < 5
```
Listing 5-31.

In this case there is no check constraint involved; both predicates are valid and each will individually return records, but they contradict each other when they are run together. As a result, the query returns no records and the plan shows a Constant Scan operator similar to the plan in Figure 5-8. This may just look like a badly written query, but remember that some predicates may already be included in, for example, view definitions, and the developer of the query may be unaware of those. For example, in Listing 5-31, a view may include the predicate `ManagerID > 10` and a developer may call the view using the predicate `ManagerID < 5`. Since both predicates contradict each other a Constant Scan operator will be used again instead.

Trivial plan

The optimization process may be expensive to initialize and run for very simple queries that don't require any cost estimation. To avoid this expensive operation for simple queries, SQL Server uses the trivial plan optimization. In short, if there's only one way, or one obvious best way to execute the query, depending on the query definition and available metadata, a lot of work can be avoided. For example, the following **Adventure-Works** query will produce a trivial plan:

```
SELECT * FROM dbo.DatabaseLog
```

Listing 5-32.

The execution plan will show if a trivial plan optimization was performed; the Optimization Level entry in the Properties window of a graphical plan will show TRIVIAL, as shown in Figure 5-9. In the same way, an XML plan will show the `StatementOptmLevel` attribute as `TRIVIAL`, as shown in the XML fragment in Listing 5-33.

```
<StmtSimple StatementOptmLevel="TRIVIAL" StatementSubTreeCost="0.471671"
StatementText="SELECT * FROM dbo.DatabaseLog;" StatementType="SELECT">
```

Listing 5-33.

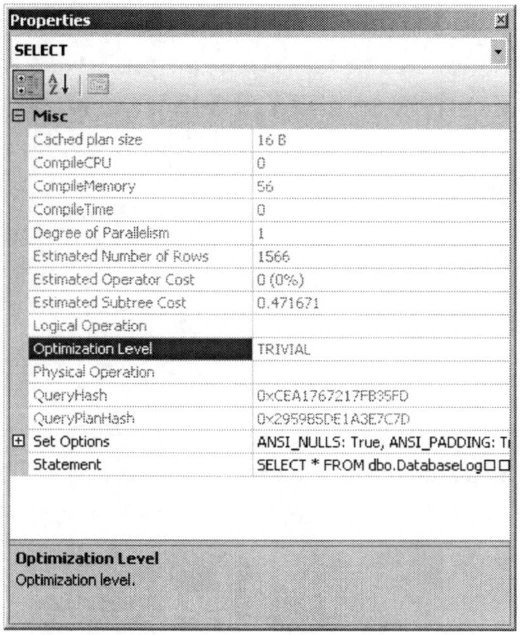

Figure 5-9: Trivial plan properties.

As I mentioned at the start of this chapter, additional information regarding the optimization process can be shown using the **sys.dm_exec_query_optimizer_info** DMV, which will produce an output similar to Table 5-1 for this query.

Counter	Occurrence	Value
elapsed time	1	0
final cost	1	0.471671267
maximum DOP	1	0

Counter	Occurrence	Value
optimizations	1	1
tables	1	1
trivial plan	1	1

Table 5-11: Optimization information for a trivial plan.

Table 5-11 shows that this was in fact a trivial plan optimization, using one table and a maximum DOP of 0, and it also displays the elapsed time and final cost. This same query was also used earlier to demonstrate the `sys.dm_exec_query_transformation_stats` DMV, which illustrated the transformation rules used by the Query Optimizer in this query, as shown previously in Listing 5-5.

The other possible value for the Optimization Level or StatementOptLevel properties is FULL, which obviously means that the query did not qualify for a trivial plan, and a full optimization was performed instead. Full optimization is used for more complicated queries or queries using more complex features, which will require comparisons of candidate plans' costs in order to guide decisions; this will be explained in the next section.

Full optimization

If a query does not qualify for a trivial plan, SQL Server will run the cost-based optimization process, which uses transformation rules to generate alternative plans, stores these alternatives in the memo structure, and uses cost estimation to select the best plan. This optimization process is executed in three stages, with different transformation rules being applied at each stage.

Since some queries may have a huge number of possible query plans, it's sometimes not feasible to explore their entire search space, as it would take too long. So, in addition to applying transformation rules, a number of heuristics are used by the Query Optimizer to control the search strategy and to limit the number of alternatives generated, in order to quickly find a good plan. The Query Optimizer needs to balance the optimization time and the quality of the selected plan. For example, as explained in *Chapter 1, Introduction to Query Optimization*, optimizing join orders can create a huge number of possible alternatives. So, a common heuristic used by SQL Server to reduce the size of the search space is to avoid considering bushy trees.

In addition, the optimization process can immediately finish if a good enough plan (relative to the Query Optimizer's internal thresholds) is found at the end of any of these three phases. However if, at the end of any given phase, the best plan is still very expensive, then the Query Optimizer will run the next phase, which will run an additional set of (usually more complex) transformation rules. These phases are shown as search 0, search 1 and search 2 on the `sys.dm_exec_query_optimizer_info` DMV.

Search 0

Similar to the concept of the trivial plan, the first phase, search 0, will aim to find a plan as quickly as possible without trying sophisticated transformations. Search 0, called the transaction processing phase, is ideal for the small queries typically found on transaction processing systems and it is used for queries with at least three tables. Before the full optimization process is started, the Query Optimizer generates the initial set of join orders based on heuristics. These heuristics begin by first joining the smallest tables or the tables that achieve the largest filtering based on their selectivity. Those are the only join orders considered on search 0. At the end of this phase, the Query Optimizer compares the cost of the best generated plan to an internal cost threshold and, if the plan is still very expensive, SQL Server will run the next phase.

Search 1

The next phase, search 1, also called Quick Plan, uses additional transformation rules, limited join reordering, and is appropriate for more complex queries. At the end of this phase, SQL Server compares the cost of the cheapest plan to a second internal cost threshold and, if the best plan is cheap enough, then the plan is selected. If the query is still expensive and the system can run parallel queries (as described in the Parallelism section in *Chapter 2, The Execution Engine*), this phase is executed again to find a good parallel plan, but no plan is selected for execution after this point. At the end of this phase, the costs of the best serial and parallel plans are compared, and the cheapest one is used in the following phase, search 2, which we'll come to in just a moment.

As an example, the following query does not qualify for search 0 and will go directly to search 1:

```
SELECT * FROM HumanResources.Employee
WHERE ManagerID = 12
```
Listing 5-34.

Using the **sys.dm_exec_query_optimizer_info** DMV as shown in Listing 5-2, you can display its optimization information seen in Table 5-12, which shows that only the search 1 phase was executed.

Counter	Occurrence	Value
elapsed time	1	0.004
final cost	1	0.00657038
maximum DOP	1	0
optimizations	1	1

Counter	Occurrence	Value
search 1	1	1
search 1 tasks	1	81
search 1 time	1	0
tables	1	1
tasks	1	81

Table 5-12:   Optimization information for search 1 phase.

The `sys.dm_exec_query_optimizer_info` DMV includes a counter named "gain stage 0 to stage 1" which shows the number of times search 1 was executed after search 0, and includes the average decrease in cost from one stage to the other, as defined by:

```
(MinimumPlanCost(search 0) - MinimumPlanCost(search 1)) / MinimumPlanCost(search 0)
```

Listing 5-35.

For example, the query we have been using before in this chapter:

```
SELECT FirstName, LastName, CustomerType
FROM Person.Contact AS C
    JOIN Sales.Individual AS I
        ON C.ContactID = I.ContactID
    JOIN Sales.Customer AS Cu
        ON I.CustomerID = Cu.CustomerID
```

Listing 5-36.

... will show the optimization information seen in Table 5-13.

Counter	Occurrence	Value
elapsed time	1	0.009
final cost	1	3.239871842
maximum DOP	1	0
optimizations	1	1
search 0 tasks	1	230
search 0 time	1	0.001
search 1	1	1
search 1 tasks	1	377
search 1 time	1	0.004
gain stage 0 to stage 1	1	0.490795403
tables	1	3
tasks	1	607

Table 5-13: Optimization information for search 0 and 1 phases.

The output shows that the optimization process went through both the search 0 and search 1 stages and that a plan was found on the latter. It also shows a cost improvement of almost 50% by going from the search 0 to the search 1 stage.

Search 2

The last phase, search 2, is called full optimization, and is used for queries ranging from complex to very complex. A larger set of the potential transformation rules, parallel operators and other advanced optimization strategies are considered in this phase and, since this is the last phase, an execution plan must be found here (perhaps with the exception of the timeout event, as explained later).

The sys.dm_exec_query_optimizer_info DMV includes another useful counter, named "gain stage 1 to stage 2," to show the number of times search 2 was executed after search 1, together with the average decrease in cost from one stage to the other, as defined by:

```
(MinimumPlanCost(search 1) — MinimumPlanCost(search 2)) / MinimumPlanCost(search 1)
```

Listing 5-37.

For example, the following query, as taken from Books Online, will create the optimization information shown in Table 5-14.[1]

```
SELECT I.CustomerID, C.FirstName, C.LastName, A.AddressLine1, A.City,
    SP.Name AS State, CR.Name AS CountryRegion
FROM Person.Contact AS C
    JOIN Sales.Individual AS I ON C.ContactID = I.ContactID
    JOIN Sales.CustomerAddress AS CA ON CA.CustomerID = I.CustomerID
    JOIN Person.Address AS A ON A.AddressID = CA.AddressID
    JOIN Person.StateProvince SP ON
        SP.StateProvinceID = A.StateProvinceID
    JOIN Person.CountryRegion CR ON
        CR.CountryRegionCode = SP.CountryRegionCode
ORDER BY I.CustomerID
```

Listing 5-38.

---

1   Output for SQL Server 2008 is shown; number of tasks will vary for SQL Server 2008 R2.

Counter	Occurrence	Value
elapsed time	I	0.166
final cost	I	5.8466425
gain stage 0 to stage 1	I	0.351461336
gain stage 1 to stage 2	I	0.002873885
indexed views matched	I	I
maximum DOP	I	0
optimizations	I	I
search 0 tasks	I	681
search 0 time	I	0.016
search 1 tasks	I	4796
search 1 time	I	0.III
search 2	I	I
search 2 tasks	I	1623
search 2 time	I	0.02
tables	I	6
tasks	I	7100

Table 5-14: Optimization information for search 2 phase.

The optimization information shows that this query went throughout all the three stages of optimization (as show in Figure 5-10) and, among other things, also includes both of the stage–to-stage gain counters described earlier.

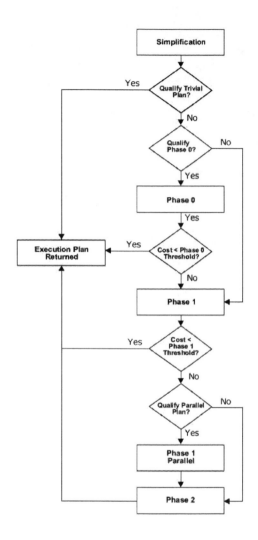

Figure 5-10: The optimization process.

As we've touched upon previously, the Query Optimizer has to find the best plan possible within the shortest amount of time. More to the point, it must eventually return a plan, even if that plan is not as efficient as it would like. To that end, the optimization process also includes the concept of a timeout value. This timeout is not a fixed amount of time, but is, instead, calculated based on the number of transformations applied together with the elapsed time.

When a timeout is found, the Query Optimizer stops the optimization process and returns the least expensive plan it has found so far. The best plan found so far could be a plan found during the current optimization stage, but most likely it would be the best plan found in the previous one. This obviously means that a timeout can happen only on the search 1 and search 2 stages; no timeouts can occur on stage 0, as the Query Optimizer needs to finish at least one optimization stage in order to find a good (or at least viable) initial plan (the same applies when stage 1 is chosen as the first optimization phase for a query). This timeout event is shown in the properties of a graphical plan as **Reason For Early Termination Of Statement Optimization**, as shown in Figure 5-11, or in an XML plan as `StatementOptmEarlyAbortReason`. This event is also shown as the timeout counter on the `sys.dm_exec_query_optimizer_info` DMV.

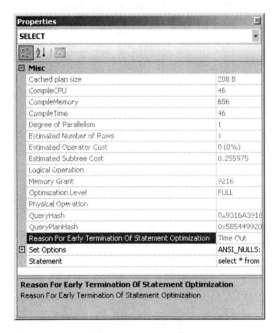

Figure 5-11: Timeout example.

Finally, at the end of the optimization process, the chosen plan will be sent to the execution engine to be run, and the results will be sent back to the client.

Summary

This chapter showed the internals of the Query Optimizer, how your query goes from a SQL statement submitted to SQL Server, all the way to the selected execution plan, including parsing, binding, simplification, trivial plan, and the full optimization stages. Important components which are part of the Query Optimizer architecture, such as transformation rules and the memo structure, were also introduced.

The Query Optimizer generates a solution space and selects the best possible execution plan from it, based on the plan cost. Transformation rules are used to generate these alternatives, which are stored in a memory structure called the memo. Instead of exploring the search space exhaustively, heuristics are also introduced to limit the number of possible solutions. Finally, the alternatives stored in the memo are costed, and the best solution is returned for execution.

Chapter 6: Additional Topics

So far we have focused on how the Query Optimizer solves `SELECT` queries with mostly joins and aggregations. In this chapter, we'll see some additional SQL features that traditionally are not covered in query optimization topics, including updates and data warehouse queries, plus some other topics related to query parameters including parameter sniffing, auto-parameterization, and forced parameterization.

Update operations are an intrinsic part of database operations, and they also need to be optimized so that they can be performed as quickly as possible. Just to be clear, when I say "updates," in truth I'm referring to any operation performed by the `INSERT`, `DELETE` or `UPDATE` statements, as well as the `MERGE` statement, which is new in SQL Server 2008. In this chapter, I'll explain the basics of update operations, and how they can quickly become complicated, as they need to update existing indexes, access multiple tables and enforce existing constraints. I will show how the Query Optimizer can select per-row and per-index plans to optimize `UPDATE` statements, and I will describe the Halloween protection problem, as well as how SQL Server avoids it.

Data warehouses are becoming increasingly popular as decision support systems for organizations of all sizes. Not only are more organizations building data warehouses, those databases are also growing in size, and multi-terabyte environments are very common today. In this chapter, I will introduce data warehousing and briefly compare it to online transaction processing systems. I will explain the basic concepts of data warehousing, including fact and dimension tables, as well as star and snowflake schemas. After that, we'll focus on how SQL Server optimizes star join queries, as well as how it can automatically detect star and snowflake schemas, and reliably identify fact and dimension tables.

We'll end the chapter with two sections discussing the use of query parameters. In the first section, I will talk about the parameter sniffing behavior and explain that, although looking at the parameters of a query helps the Query Optimizer to produce better execution plans, the occasional reuse of some of these plans can also be a performance problem. I will demonstrate how you can identify problems related to the parameter sniffing behavior, and I will provide a few recommendations on how to avoid them, including the use of the **OPTIMIZE FOR** or **RECOMPILE** hints. Finally, the auto-parameterization behavior is explained, along with forced parameterization, a more drastic choice to parameterize queries, which was introduced with SQL Server 2005.

Updates

Even when performing an update involves some other areas of SQL Server, such as transactions, concurrency control or locking, update processing is still totally integrated within the SQL Server query processor framework. Update operations are also optimized so they can be performed as quickly as possible. So, in this section I will talk about updates from the point of view of the Query Optimizer. As mentioned earlier, for the purposes of this section, I'll refer to any operation performed by the **INSERT**, **DELETE**, **UPDATE**, or **MERGE** statements as updates.

Update plans can be complicated, as they need to update existing indexes alongside data and, because of objects like check constraints, referential integrity constraints and triggers, those plans may also have to access multiple tables and enforce existing constraints. Updates may also require the updating of multiple tables when cascading referential integrity constraints or triggers are defined. Some of these operations, such as updating indexes, can have a big impact on the performance of the entire update operation, and we'll take a deeper look at that now.

Update operations are performed in two steps, which can be summarized as a read section followed by the update section. The first step provides the details of the changes to apply and which records will be updated. For **INSERT** operations, this includes the values to be inserted and, for **DELETE** operations, it includes obtaining the keys of the records to be deleted, which could be the clustering keys for clustered indexes or the RIDs for heaps. Just to keep you on your toes, for update operations, a combination of both the keys of the records to be updated and the data to be inserted is needed. In this first step, SQL Server may read the table to be updated just like in any other SELECT statement.

In the second step, the update operations are performed, including updating indexes, validating constraints and executing triggers. The update operation will fail and roll back if it violates a constraint.

Let me start with an example of a very simple update operation. Inserting a new record on the **Person.CountryRegion** table using the next query creates a very simple plan, as shown in Figure 6-1.

```
INSERT INTO Person.CountryRegion (CountryRegionCode, Name) VALUES ('ZZ', 'New
Country')
```
Listing 6-1.

```
INSERT          Clustered Index Insert
Cost: 0 %           Cost: 100 %
```

Figure 6-1:   An insert example.

However, the same scenario gets complicated very quickly when you try to delete the same record by running the next statement, as shown on the plan in Figure 6-2.

```
DELETE FROM Person.CountryRegion
WHERE CountryRegionCode = 'ZZ'
```
Listing 6-2.

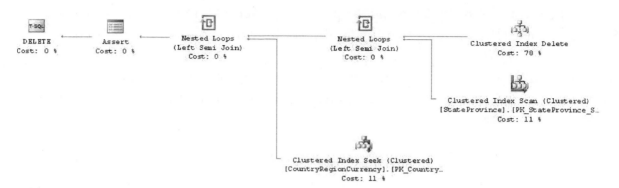

Figure 6-2: A delete example.

As you can see in this plan, in addition to `CountryRegion`, two additional tables (`StateProvince` and `CountryRegionCurrency`) are accessed. The reason behind this is that these two tables have a foreign key referencing `CountryRegion`, and so SQL Server needs to validate that no records exist on these tables for this specific value of `CountryRegionCode`. So, the tables are accessed, and an Assert operator is included at the end of the plan to perform this validation. If a record with the `CountryRegionCode` to be deleted exists in any of these tables, the Assert operator will throw an exception and SQL Server will roll back the transaction, returning the following error message:

```
Msg 547, Level 16, State 0, Line 2
The DELETE statement conflicted with the REFERENCE constraint "FK_StateProvince_CountryRegion_
CountryRegionCode." The conflict occurred in database "AdventureWorks," table "Person.
StateProvince," column 'CountryRegionCode'.
```

Listing 6-3.

So as you can see, the previous example showed how update operations can access some other tables not included in the original query, in this case, because of the definition of referential integrity constraints. The updating of non-clustered indexes is covered in the next section.

Per-row and per-index plans

An important operation performed by updates is the modifying and updating of existing non-clustered indexes, which is done by using per-row or per-index maintenance plans (also called narrow and wide plans, respectively). In a per-row maintenance plan, the updates to the base table and the existing indexes are performed by a single operator, one row at a time. On the other hand, in a per-index maintenance plan, the base table and each non-clustered index are updated in separated operations.

Except for a few cases where per-index plans are mandatory, the Query Optimizer can choose between a per-row and per-index plan based on performance reasons, and on an index-by-index basis. Although factors like the structure and size of the table, as well as the other operations performed by the UPDATE statement, are all considered, choosing between per-index and per-row plans will mostly depend on the number of records being updated. The Query Optimizer is more likely to choose a per-row plan when a small number of records are being updated, and a per-index plan when the number of records to be updated increases, as this choice scales better. A drawback with the per-row approach is that the storage engine updates the non-clustered index rows using the clustered index key order, which is not efficient when a large number of records need to be updated.

The query in Listing 6-4 will create a per-row plan, which is shown in Figure 6-3 (two additional queries may be shown on the plan due to the execution of an existing trigger).

Note

The following two queries delete data from the AdventureWorks database, so perhaps you should request an estimated plan if you don't want the records to be deleted. Alternatively, you could perform a database backup before running these queries, so that you will be able to restore the database later.

```
DELETE FROM Sales.SalesOrderDetail
WHERE SalesOrderDetailID = 61130
```

Listing 6-4.

Figure 6-3: A per-row plan.

In addition to updating the clustered index, this delete operation will update two existing non-clustered indexes, `IX_SalesOrderDetail_ProductID` and `AK_SalesOrder-Detail_rowguid`, which can be seen listed on the Object property in the Properties window of the Clustered Index Delete operator, as shown in Figure 6-4.

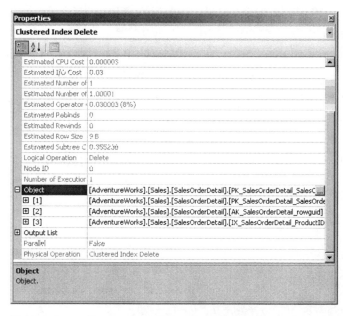

Figure 6-4: Properties of the Clustered Index Delete operator.

When a large number of records are being updated, the Query Optimizer may choose a per-index plan, which the following query will demonstrate, by creating the per-index plan shown in Figures 6-5 and 6-6.

```
DELETE FROM Sales.SalesOrderDetail
WHERE SalesOrderDetailID < 43740
```

Listing 6-5.

In a per-index update, the base table is updated first, which is shown by the Clustered Index Delete operator in Figure 6-5.

In the second part of the plan, which is shown in Figure 6-6, a Table Spool operator is used to read the data of the key values of the indexes to be updated, and then a Sort operator sorts the data in the order of the index. Later, an Index Delete operator updates a specific non-clustered index in one operation (the name of which you can see on the graphical plan). Although, the table spool is listed twice in the plan, it is actually the same operator being reused. Finally, the Sequence operator makes sure that each Index Delete operation is performed in sequence, as shown from top to bottom.

Figure 6-5: Right part of the per-index plan.

Figure 6-6: Left part of the per-index plan.

In summary, keep in mind that, except for a few cases where per-index plans are mandatory, the Query Optimizer can choose between a per-row and per-index plan on an index-by-index basis, so it is even possible to have both maintenance choices in the same execution plan.

Halloween protection

Halloween protection refers to a problem which appears in certain update operations, and which was found more than thirty years ago by researchers working on the System R project (mentioned in *Chapter 1, Introduction to Query Optimization*) at the IBM Almaden Research Center. The System R team was testing a query optimizer when they ran a query to update the salary column on an `Employee` table. The query was supposed to give a 10% raise to every employee with a salary of less than $25,000 but, to their surprise, no employee had a salary under $25,000 after the update query was completed. They noticed that the query optimizer had selected the salary index and had updated some records multiple times, until they reached the $25,000 salary. Since the salary index was used to scan the records, when the salary column was updated, some records were moved within the index and were then scanned again later, updating those records more than once. The problem was called Halloween problem simply because it was discovered on Halloween around 1976 or 1977.

As I mentioned at the beginning of this section, update operations have a read section followed by an update section, and that is a crucial distinction to bear in mind at this stage. To avoid the Halloween problem, the read and update sections must be completely separated; the read section must be completed in its entirety before the write section is run. I'll show you how SQL Server avoids the Halloween problem in the next example. Run the statement in Listing 6-6 to create a new table.

```
SELECT *
INTO dbo.Product
FROM Production.Product
```

Listing 6-6.

Run the following **UPDATE** statement, which produces the execution plan on Figure 6-7.

```
UPDATE dbo.Product
SET ListPrice = ListPrice * 1.2
```

Listing 6-7.

Figure 6-7: An update without Halloween protection.

No Halloween protection is needed in this case, as the statement updates the **ListPrice** column, which is not part of any index, and so updating the data does not move any rows around. Now, to demonstrate the problem, I'll create a clustered index on **ListPrice** column.

```
CREATE CLUSTERED INDEX cix ON dbo.Product(ListPrice)
```

Listing 6-8.

Run the same **UPDATE** statement from Listing 6-7 again. The query will show a similar plan, but this time including a Table Spool operator, which is a blocking operator, separating the read section from the write section. A blocking operator has to read *all* of the relevant rows before producing any output rows to the next operator. In this example, the table spool separates the Clustered Index Scan from the Clustered Index Update, as shown in Figure 6-8.

The spool operator scans the original data and saves a copy of it in a hidden spool table in tempdb before it is updated. A Table Spool operator is usually used to avoid the Halloween problem as it is a cheap operator. However, if the plan already includes another operator that can be used, such as a Sort, then the Table Spool operator is not needed, and the Sort can perform the same blocking job instead.

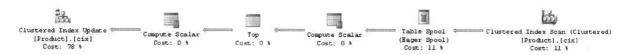

Figure 6-8:   An update with Halloween protection.

Finally, drop the table you have just created.

```
DROP TABLE dbo.Product
```

Listing 6-9.

Data Warehouses

A data warehouse is a decision support system for business decision making, designed to execute queries from users as well as running reporting and analytical applications. It is also structurally different from an online transaction processing (OLTP) system, which focuses on operational transaction processing (we'll look at some of these differences in a just a moment). Because of these different purposes, both systems also have different workloads: a data warehouse will usually have to support complex and large queries, compared to the typically small transactions of an OLTP system.

Another main difference between OLTP databases and data warehouses is the degree of normalization found in them. An OLTP system uses normalized databases, usually at a third normal form, while a data warehouse uses a denormalized dimensional model. An OLTP normalized model helps to remove data redundancies,and focus on data integrity; it benefits update operations as data needs to be updated in one place only. On the other hand, a data warehouse dimensional model is more appropriate for ad hoc complex queries, and will usually have fewer tables and require fewer joins.

Dimensional data modeling on data warehouses relies on the use of fact and dimension tables. Fact tables contain facts or numerical measures of the business, which can participate in calculations, while dimension tables are the attributes or descriptions of the facts. Fact tables also usually have foreign keys to link them to the primary keys of the dimension tables.

Data warehouses also usually follow star and snowflake schema structures. A star schema contains a fact table and a single table for each dimension. Snowflake schemas are similar to star schemas to the extent that they also have a fact table but, in addition, dimension tables can also be normalized, and each dimension can have more than one table. Fact tables are typically huge and can store millions or billions of rows, compared to dimension tables, which are significantly smaller. The size of data warehouse databases tends to range from hundreds of gigabytes to terabytes.

SQL Server sample databases includes AdventureWorksDW, a data warehouse database whose purpose is to demonstrate the SQL Server business intelligence features. The AdventureWorksDW database will be used for the example in this section.

Queries that join a fact table to dimension tables are called star join queries. SQL Server includes special optimizations for star join queries (which we'll look at shortly), can automatically detect star and snowflake schemas, and can reliably identify fact and dimension tables. This is significant because sometimes, in order to avoid the overhead of constraint enforcement during updates, data warehouse implementations don't explicitly define foreign key constraints. In these cases, the Query Optimizer may need to rely on heuristics to detect star schemas.

One such heuristic is to consider the largest table of the star join query as the fact table (which, in addition, must have a specified minimum size, currently defined as 100 pages). The second heuristic requires that all the joins in a star join query need to be inner joins, and use equality predicates on a single column. It should also be noticed that even in the rare case where a dimension table is incorrectly chosen as a fact table through the use of these heuristics, the Query Optimizer will still select a valid plan which will return the correct data, although it may not be an efficient one.

Regarding optimizations for star join queries, it is interesting to consider the use of Cartesian (or Cross) products of the dimension tables with multi-column index lookups on a fact table. Although Cross products are avoided during the regular optimization process because they can generate huge intermediate results, they can be used for data warehouse queries involving small dimension tables. As the rows of the Cross product are being generated, they are immediately used to look up on a multi-column index without requiring a lot of memory for the intermediate results.

In *Optimizing Star Join Queries for Data Warehousing in Microsoft SQL Server*,[1] Cesar Galindo-Legaria et al. define three different approaches to optimizing star join queries based on the selectivity of the fact table, as shown next. As mentioned in *Chapter 3, Statistics and Cost Estimation*, selectivity is a measure of the number of records that are estimated to be returned by a query and, slightly anti-intuitively, smaller numbers represent higher selectivity (i.e. fewer rows).

For highly selective queries which return up to 10% of the rows in the fact table, the Query Optimizer may produce a plan with Nested Loops Joins, Index Seeks and bookmark lookups. For medium selectivity queries, which return anywhere from 10 to 75% of the records in the fact table, SQL Server may recommend Hash Joins with bitmap filters in combination with fact table scans or fact table range scans. Finally, for the least selective queries, processing more than 75% of the fact table, the Query Optimizer mostly will recommend regular Hash Joins with fact table scans. The choice of these operators

---

[1] Published in the Proceedings of the 2008 IEEE 24th International Conference on Data Engineering.

and plans is not surprising for the highly and least selective queries, as it is their standard usage as explained in *Chapter 2, The Execution Engine*. What is new is the choice of Hash Joins and bitmap filtering for medium selectivity queries, so that's what we'll look at next.

Bitmap filtering is an optimization for star join queries that was introduced with SQL Server 2008 and it is only available on the Enterprise, Developer and Evaluation editions. It is referred to as optimized bitmap filtering in order to differentiate it from the standard bitmap filtering which was already available in previous versions of SQL Server. Optimized bitmap filtering improves the performance of star join queries by removing unnecessary rows from processing early in the query plan, so that subsequent operators have fewer rows to process. In our case, it filters rows from the fact table to avoid additional join processing.

This strategy is called "semi-join reduction" and relies on the fact that only the records from the second table that qualify for the join with the first table are processed. SQL Server bitmap filters are based on bloom filters, originally conceived by Burton Bloom in 1970. Other semi-join reduction technologies like bitmap indexes have been used by other database vendors.

Optimized bitmap filtering works with Hash Joins which (as we saw in Chapter 2) use two inputs, the smaller of which (the build table) is being completely read into memory. Optimized bitmap filtering takes advantage of the fact that a Hash Join has to process the build input anyway so, as SQL Server is processing the build table, it creates a bitmap representation of the join key values found. Since SQL Server can reliably detect fact and dimension tables, and the latter are almost always the smaller of the two, the build input upon which the bitmap is based will be a dimension table. This bitmap representation of the dimension table will be used to filter the second input of the Hash Join, the probe input, which in this case will be the fact table. This basically means that only the rows in the fact table that qualify for the join to the dimension table will be processed.

Next, let's see an example of optimized bitmap filtering. Run the query in Listing 6-10.

```
USE AdventureWorksDW
GO
SELECT *
FROM dbo.FactInternetSales AS f
JOIN dbo.DimProduct AS p ON f.ProductKey = p.ProductKey
JOIN dbo.DimCustomer AS c ON f.CustomerKey = c.CustomerKey
WHERE p.ListPrice > 50 AND c.Gender = 'M'
```

Listing 6-10.

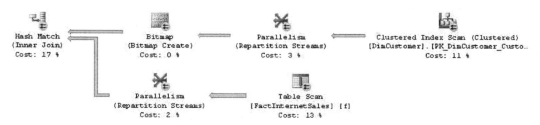

Figure 6-9: A bitmap filtering example.

Note

You may not get the plan shown earlier on a test system with a limited number of logical processors, but you can simulate that your SQL Server instance has (for example) 8 processors by using the –P startup parameter. In order to do that, open **Configuration Manager,** *right-click on your SQL Server service, select* **Properties,** *select the* **Advanced** *tab, and edit the* **Startup Parameters** *entry by adding ";-P8" at the end of the line. Click* **OK** *and restart the instance, remembering to remove this entry when you finish your testing.*

Since this plan is too big to show here, only a section is included in Figure 6-9 (this plan was created with SQL Server 2008 R2, so the one for SQL Server 2008 may vary a little). This part of the plan shows one of the two available Bitmap operators, in this case processing the rows from the DimCustomer table, which is the build input of the Hash

Join shown on the left. This Bitmap operator is identified as `Opt_Bitmap1007`, as you can verify in the operator's Properties window, and the `Opt_` prefix indicates that optimized bitmap filtering is, in fact, being used. The second Bitmap operator, not shown on this part of the plan, is identified as `Opt_Bitmap1008`. The probe input of the Hash Join is a Table Scan operator on the `FactInternetSales` fact table, which is also shown in Figure 6-9. Finally, the predicate section of this Table Scan operator's properties, as shown in Figure 6-10, shows that both the `Opt_Bitmap1007` and `Opt_Bitmap1008` bitmap filters are being applied to the fact table to remove non-qualifying rows before the Hash Join.

Table Scan
Scan rows from a table.

Physical Operation	Table Scan
Logical Operation	Table Scan
Estimated I/O Cost	0.846907
Estimated CPU Cost	0.0166291
Estimated Number of Executions	1
Estimated Operator Cost	0.863536 (13%)
Estimated Subtree Cost	0.863536
Estimated Number of Rows	60398
Estimated Row Size	195 B
Ordered	False
Node ID	12

Predicate
PROBE([Opt_Bitmap1007],[AdventureWorksDW].[dbo].
[FactInternetSales].[CustomerKey] as [F].
[CustomerKey],N'[IN ROW]') AND PROBE
([Opt_Bitmap1008],[AdventureWorksDW].[dbo].
[FactInternetSales].[ProductKey] as [F].
[ProductKey],N'[IN ROW]')
Object
[AdventureWorksDW].[dbo].[FactInternetSales] [F]

Figure 6-10: Fact table Table Scan operator properties.

Finally, bitmap filtering can significantly improve the performance of data warehouse queries by pushing the filters down into the scan of the fact table early in the query plan, so that subsequent operators have fewer rows to process.

Parameter Sniffing

As we saw in *Chapter 3, Statistics and Cost Estimation*, SQL Server can use the histograms of statistics objects to estimate the cardinality of a query, and then use this information to try to produce an optimal execution plan. The Query Optimizer accomplishes this by first inspecting the values of the query parameters.

This behavior is called parameter sniffing, and it is a very good thing: getting an execution plan tailored to the current parameters of a query naturally improves the performance of your applications. We also know that the plan cache can store these execution plans so that they can be reused the next time the same query needs to be executed. This saves optimization time and CPU resources, as the query does not need to be optimized again.

However, although the Query Optimizer and the plan cache work well together most of the time, some performance problems can occasionally appear. Given that the Query Optimizer can produce different execution plans for syntactically identical queries, depending on their parameters, caching and reusing only one of these plans may create a performance issue for alternative instances of this query which would benefit from a better plan. This is a known problem with queries using explicit parameterization, such as stored procedures, for example. Next, I'll show you an example of this problem, together with a few recommendations on how to fix it.

Let's write a simple stored procedure using the `Sales.SalesOrderDetail` table on the `AdventureWorks` database:

```
CREATE PROCEDURE test (@pid int)
AS
SELECT * FROM Sales.SalesOrderDetail
WHERE ProductID = @pid
```

Listing 6-11.

Run the following statement to execute the stored procedure, and request to display the execution plan:

```
EXEC test @pid = 897
```

Listing 6-12.

The Query Optimizer estimates that only a few records will be returned by this query, and produces the execution plan shown in Figure 6-11, which uses an Index Seek operator to quickly find the records on an existing non-clustered index, and a Key Lookup operator to search on the base table for the remaining columns requested by the query.

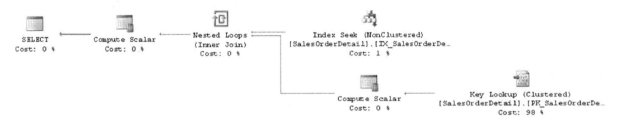

Figure 6-11: Plan using Index Seek and Key Lookup operators.

This combination of Index Seek and Key Lookup operators was a good choice because, although it's a relatively expensive combination, the query was highly selective. However, what if a different parameter is used, producing a less selective predicate? For example, try the following query, including a SET STATISTICS IO ON statement to display the amount of disk activity generated by the query:

```
SET STATISTICS IO ON
GO
EXEC test @pid = 870
GO
```

Listing 6-13.

The Messages tab will show an output similar to the one in Listing 6-14.

```
Table 'SalesOrderDetail'. Scan count 1, logical reads 15615, physical reads 87, read-ahead
reads 150, …
```
Listing 6-14.

As you can see, on this execution alone, SQL Server is performing 15,615 logical reads when the base table only has 1,244 pages; so it's using over 12 times more I/Os than just simply scanning the entire table. As we have seen before, performing Index Seeks plus Key Lookups to the base table, which uses random I/Os, is a very expensive operation.

Now clear the plan cache to remove the execution plan currently held in memory, and run the stored procedure again, using the same parameter as in Listing 6-13.

```
DBCC FREEPROCCACHE
GO
EXEC test @pid = 870
GO
```
Listing 6-15.

This time, you'll get a totally different execution plan. The I/O information now will show that only around 1,240 pages were read, and the execution plan will include a Clustered Index Scan as shown in Figure 6-12. Since, this time, there was no optimized version of the stored procedure stored in the plan cache, SQL Server optimized it from scratch using the new parameter, and created a new optimal execution plan.

Figure 6-12: Plan using a Clustered Index Scan.

Of course, this doesn't mean that you're not supposed to trust your stored procedures any more, or that maybe all your code is incorrect. This is just a problem that you need to be aware of and research, especially if you have queries where performance changes dramatically when different parameters are introduced. If you happen to have this problem, there are a few choices available, which we'll explore now.

Optimize for a typical parameter

There might be cases when most of the executions of a query use the same execution plan and you want to avoid an ongoing optimization cost. In these cases you can use the **OPTIMIZE FOR** hint, which helps when an optimal plan is generated for the majority of values used in a specific parameter. As a result, only the few executions using an atypical parameter will not have an optimal plan.

Suppose that almost all of the executions of our stored procedure would benefit from the previous plan using an Index Seek and a Key Lookup operator. To take advantage of that, you could write the stored procedure as in Listing 6-16.

```
ALTER PROCEDURE test (@pid int)
AS
SELECT * FROM Sales.SalesOrderDetail
WHERE ProductID = @pid
OPTION (OPTIMIZE FOR (@pid = 897))
```

Listing 6-16.

When you run the stored procedure for the first time, it will be optimized for the value 897, no matter what parameter value was actually specified for the execution. If you want check, test the case in Listing 6-17.

```
EXEC test @pid = 870
```

Listing 6-17.

You can find the following entry close to the end of the XML plan.

```
<ParameterList>
<ColumnReference Column="@pid" ParameterCompiledValue="(897)"
ParameterRuntimeValue="(870)" />
</ParameterList>
```

Listing 6-18.

This entry clearly shows which parameter value was used during optimization, and which one was used during execution. In this case, the stored procedure is optimized only once, and the plan is stored in the plan cache and reused as many times as needed. The benefit of using this hint, in addition to avoiding optimization cost, is that you have total control over which plan is stored in the plan cache.

Optimize on every execution

If you want the best performance for every query, the solution might be to optimize for every execution. You will get the best possible plan on every execution but will end up paying for the optimization cost, so you'll need to decide if that's a worthwhile trade-off. To do this, use the **RECOMPILE** hint as shown in Listing 6-19.

```
ALTER PROCEDURE test (@pid int)
AS
SELECT * FROM Sales.SalesOrderDetail
WHERE ProductID = @pid
OPTION (RECOMPILE)
```

Listing 6-19.

The XML plan for this execution:

```
EXEC test @pid = 897
```

Listing 6-20.

... will show:

```
<ParameterList>
<ColumnReference Column="@pid" ParameterCompiledValue="(897)"
ParameterRuntimeValue="(897)" />
</ParameterList>
```

Listing 6-21.

Local Variables and OPTIMIZE FOR UNKNOWN

Another solution that has been traditionally implemented in the past is the use of local variables instead of parameters. As mentioned in *Chapter 3, Statistics and Cost Estimation*, SQL Server is not able to see the values of local variables at optimization time, as these values are only known at execution time. However, by using local variables you are not only disabling parameter sniffing, you're also disabling the Query Optimizer's option of using the statistics histogram to find an optimal plan for the query. Instead, it will rely on just the density information of the statistics object, as explained in Chapter 3.

This solution will simply ignore the parameter values and use the same execution plan for all the executions, but at least you're getting a consistent plan every time. A variation of the OPTIMIZE FOR hint shown previously, OPTIMIZE FOR UNKNOWN, which was introduced with SQL Server 2008, has the same effect.

Running the following two versions of our stored procedure will have equivalent outcomes, and will produce the same execution plan. The first version uses local variables, and the second one uses the new `OPTIMIZE FOR UNKNOWN` hint.

```
ALTER PROCEDURE test (@pid int)
AS
DECLARE @p int = @pid
SELECT * FROM Sales.SalesOrderDetail
WHERE ProductID = @p
```

Listing 6-22.

```
ALTER PROCEDURE test (@pid int)
AS
SELECT * FROM Sales.SalesOrderDetail
WHERE ProductID = @pid
OPTION (OPTIMIZE FOR UNKNOWN)
```

Listing 6-23.

In this case, the Query Optimizer will create the plan using the Clustered Index Scan shown previously.

Auto-parameterization

The Query Optimizer might decide to parameterize queries in those cases where the value of a specific parameter does not impact the choice of an execution plan. That is, in the cases where it does not matter which parameter value is used, the plan returned will be the same.

This is a very conservative policy and SQL Server will only use it when it is safe to do so, and the performance of the queries will not be negatively impacted. In this case, the parameterized plan can be reused by similar queries which differ only in the value of their parameters. This feature, which helps to avoid optimization time and cost, is called auto-parameterization, and was introduced with SQL Server 7.0.

For example, the next two SQL statements, which were introduced as part of a stored procedure in Listing 6-22, will produce different execution plans and will not be parameterized, even when the queries are syntactically identical and only the parameters are different. In this case, the Query Optimizer decides that it isn't safe to auto-parameterize them (and thereby reuse an existing execution plan).

```
SELECT * FROM Sales.SalesOrderDetail
WHERE ProductID = 897
```

Listing 6-24.

```
SELECT * FROM Sales.SalesOrderDetail
WHERE ProductID = 870
```

Listing 6-25.

On the other hand, the following query *will* be auto-parameterized:

```
SELECT * FROM Sales.SalesOrderHeader
WHERE SalesOrderID = 43669
```

Listing 6-26.

In this case, the `SalesOrderID` column is the primary key of the `SalesOrderHeader` table, so it is guaranteed to be unique. In addition, the query predicate is using an equality operator, so there will always be a maximum of one record returned. Given these factors, SQL Server decides that it is safe to parameterize this plan by using a Clustered Index Seek operator. You can verify if your query is using a parameterized plan by inspecting the plan cache, as in the query shown in Listing 6-27.

```
SELECT text
FROM sys.dm_exec_cached_plans
CROSS APPLY sys.dm_exec_sql_text(plan_handle)
WHERE text LIKE '%SalesOrderID%'
```
Listing 6-27.

The output will include the following auto-parameterized query which will show placeholders like @1 for the parameter values:

```
(@1 int)SELECT * FROM [Sales].[SalesOrderHeader] WHERE [SalesOrderID]=@1
```
Listing 6-28.

Forced parameterization

Finally, a new feature, called forced parameterization, was introduced in SQL Server 2005 to parameterize queries more aggressively. This feature is disabled by default and can be enabled at the database level, or it can be used on an individual query by using the PARAMETERIZATION FORCED query hint.

By enabling forced parameterization you can reduce the frequency of query optimizations, but you may also introduce suboptimal plans for some instances of those queries, so you should do extensive analysis and testing of your application to verify that your performance is, in fact, being improved. To differentiate it from forced parameterization, auto-parameterization is also referred to as simple parameterization. For more information about forced parameterization please consult Books Online.

To show how forced parameterization works, execute the statement in Listing 6-29 to enable forced parameterization at the database level.

```
ALTER DATABASE AdventureWorks SET PARAMETERIZATION FORCED
```

Listing 6-29.

With this new configuration, the two queries in Listings 6-24 and 6-25, which returned two distinct execution plans, will now be parameterized and produce only one plan. Run the following query again:

```
SELECT * FROM Sales.SalesOrderDetail
WHERE ProductID = 897
```

Listing 6-30.

Because of the parameter used on this instance of the query, SQL Server will create a plan using an Index Seek and a Key Lookup, which may be used by any similar query. Of course, the risk for this specific example is that the first query will get a plan which is tailored to its parameters, but which may be suboptimal for some other instances of the same query with different parameters (like the ProductID 870 query used in Listing 6-25). Run the following query to verify that the plan was, in fact, parameterized:

```
SELECT text
FROM sys.dm_exec_cached_plans
CROSS APPLY sys.dm_exec_sql_text(plan_handle)
WHERE text LIKE '%Sales%'
```

Listing 6-31.

It will show an output similar to this:

```
(@0 int)select * from Sales . SalesOrderDetail where ProductID = @0
```

Listing 6-32.

Finally, do not forget to set parameterization back to its default value by running the following statement:

```
ALTER DATABASE AdventureWorks SET PARAMETERIZATION SIMPLE
```

Listing 6-33.

Summary

The focus of the book so far has been on optimizing **SELECT** queries with joins and aggregates. This chapter is the first time we've considered additional optimization topics related to updates, data warehousing, parameter sniffing and auto-parameterization. We've seen how the Query Optimizer decides between per-row and per-index plans to optimize **UPDATE** statements, and we've examined how updates need to perform additional operations like updating existing indexes, accessing additional tables, and enforcing existing constraints.

Basic data warehousing concepts, including fact and dimension tables as well as star and snowflake schemas, were introduced, with the focus being on how SQL Server optimizes star join queries. Some optimizations, such as Cross products of dimension tables with multi-column index lookups, and bitmap filtering, were also explained.

We've ended the chapter with topics related to the use of query parameters, and how they affect both the query optimization process and the reuse of plans by the plan cache. Topics like parameter sniffing, auto-parameterization and forced parameterization have also been introduced.

Chapter 7: Hints

SQL is a declarative language; it only defines *what* data to retrieve from the database. It doesn't describe the manner in which the data should be fetched. That, as we know, is the job of the Query Optimizer, which analyzes a number of candidate execution plans for a given query, estimates the cost of each of these plans, and selects an efficient plan by choosing the cheapest of the choices considered.

But there may be cases when the execution plan selected is not performing as you have expected and, as part of your query troubleshooting process, you may try to find a better plan yourself. Before doing this, keep in mind that, just because your query does not perform as you have expected, that does not mean that a better plan is always possible. Your plan may be an efficient one, but this is, in fact, probably an expensive query to perform, or your system may be having performance bottlenecks which are impacting the query execution.

However, although the Query Optimizer does an excellent job most of the time, it does occasionally fail to produce an efficient plan, as we've seen throughout this book. That being said, even in the cases when you're not getting an efficient plan, you should still try to distinguish between the times when the problems arise because you're not providing the Query Optimizer with all the information it needs to do a good job, and those when the problems are a result of a Query Optimizer limitation. Part of the focus of this book so far has been to help you to provide the Query Optimizer with the information it needs to produce an efficient execution plan, such as the right indexes or good quality statistics, and also how to troubleshoot the cases when you are not getting a good plan. This chapter will cover what to do if you hit a Query Optimizer limitation.

Having said that, there might be cases when the Query Optimizer just gets it wrong and, in such cases, we may be forced to resort to the use of **hints**. These are essentially optimizer directives which allow us to take explicit control over the execution plan for a given query, with the goal of improving its performance. In reaching for a hint, however, we are going against the declarative property of the SQL language and, instead, giving direct instructions to the Query Optimizer. Overriding the Query Optimizer is a risky business; hints need to be used with caution, and only as a last resort when no other option is available to produce a viable plan.

With this warning in mind, this chapter will review some of the hints that SQL Server provides, should the need arise, as well as how and when they might be used. It does *not* attempt to provide comprehensive coverage; indeed, we'll focus only on those hints I've most often seen provide positive performance benefits in certain circumstances, and we'll look at those in a few pages. Some other query hints, like `OPTIMIZE FOR`, `OPTIMIZE FOR UNKNOWN` and `RECOMPILE` have already been covered in the Parameter Sniffing section of Chapter 6, and will not be touched upon again in this chapter.

Before You Reach for a Hint...

Hints are a powerful means by which we can cause our decisions to overrule those of the Query Optimizer. However, we should only do so with extreme caution, because hints restrict the choices available to the Query Optimizer, will make your code less flexible, and will require additional maintenance. A hint should only be employed once you're certain that you have no alternative options. As a minimum, before you reach for a hint, you should explore the potential issues below.

- **Check for system problems** – You need to make sure that your performance problem is not linked to other system-related issues, such as blocking, or bottlenecks in server resources such as I/O, memory, or CPU.

- **Check for cardinality estimation errors** – The Query Optimizer often misses the correct plan because of cardinality estimation errors. Cardinality estimation errors can be detected using the `SET STATISTICS PROFILE ON` statement, and can often be fixed using solutions like updating statistics, using a bigger sample for your statistics (or scanning the entire table), using computed columns, or filtered statistics, etc. There might be cases where the cardinality estimation errors are caused by the use of features in which statistics are not supported at all, such as table variables or multi-statement table-valued functions. In these particular instances you may consider using standard or temporary tables if you are not getting an efficient plan. Statistics and cardinality estimation errors are covered in more detail in *Chapter 3, Statistics and Cost Estimation*.

- **Additional troubleshooting** – You may need to perform additional troubleshooting before considering the use of hints. One of the obvious choices for improving the performance of your queries is providing the Query Optimizer with the right indexes. How to make sure that your indexes are selected by the Query Optimizer is covered in *Chapter 4, Index Selection*. You might also consider some other, less obvious trouble-shooting procedures, like partitioning your query into steps or smaller pieces and storing any intermediate results in temporary tables. Temporary tables can give you the benefit of additional statistics which can help the Query Optimizer to produce more efficient plans. You can use this method just as a troubleshooting procedure, for example, to find out which part of the original query is expensive, so you can focus on it. Alternatively, you can keep it as the final version of your query if these changes alone give you better performance.

As discussed in this book's introduction, query optimizers have improved radically after more than 30 years of research, but still face some technical challenges. The SQL Server Query Optimizer will give you an efficient execution plan for most of your queries, but will be increasingly challenged as the complexity of the query grows with more tables joined, plus the use of aggregations, and other SQL features.

If, after investigating the troubleshooting options and recommendations described above and throughout this book, you still find that the Query Optimizer is not finding a good execution plan for your query, then you may need to consider using hints to direct the Query Optimizer toward what you feel is the optimal execution path.

Always remember that, by applying a hint, you effectively disable some of the available transformation rules to which the Query Optimizer usually has access, and so restrict the available search space. Only transformation rules that help to achieve the requested plan will be executed. For example, if you use hints to force a particular join order, the Query Optimizer will disable rules that reorder joins. Always try to use the least restrictive hint, as this will retain as much flexibility as possible in your query, and make maintenance somewhat easier. In addition, hints can not be used to generate an invalid plan or a plan that the Query Optimizer normally would not consider during query optimization.

Furthermore, a hint that initially does a great job might actively hinder performance at a later point in time when some conditions change; for example, as a result of schema updates, service packs, new versions of SQL Server, or even enough data changes. The hints may prevent the Query Optimizer from modifying the execution plan accordingly, and thus result in degraded performance. It is *your* responsibility to monitor and maintain your hinted queries to make sure that they continue to perform well after such system changes or, even better, to remove them if they are no longer needed.

Plan guides

Plan guides can help in this scenario as they allow you to apply hints without changing the text of the query directly. They separate the hint specification from the query itself, and so are an excellent choice for applying a hint, or even specifying an entire plan, that can then be easily removed in the future. This makes them particularly useful when dealing with third-party application code, or if you simply want to apply hints in a more easily maintainable way. There is a whole section dedicated to exploring plan guides, at the end of this chapter.

Remember, also, that if you decide to use a hint to change a single section or physical operator of a plan, then after applying the hint, the Query Optimizer will perform a completely new optimization. The Query Optimizer will obey your hint during the optimization process, but it still has the flexibility to change everything else in the plan, so the end result of your tweaking may be unintended changes to other sections of the plan.

Finally, note that the Query Optimizer cannot perform miracles. The fact that your query is not performing as you hoped does not always mean that the Query Optimizer is not giving you the best possible execution plan. If the operation you are performing is simply expensive and resource intensive, then it's possible that no amount of tuning or hinting will help you achieve the performance you'd like.

Types of Hints

SQL Server provides a wide range of hints which can be classified as follows:

- **query hints** tell the optimizer to apply "this hint" throughout the entire query and are specified using the OPTION clause, which is included at the end of the query

- **join hints** apply to a specific join in a query, and can be specified by using the ANSI-style join hints

- **table hints** apply to a single table and are usually included using the WITH keyword on the FROM clause.

Another useful classification is dividing hints into physical operator and goal oriented hints. Physical operator hints, as the name suggests, request the use of a specific physical operator, join order or aggregation placement. On the other hand, a goal oriented hint does not specify how to build the plan, but instead specifies a goal to achieve, leaving the Query Optimizer to find the best physical operators to achieve that goal. Goal oriented hints are usually safer and require less knowledge about the internal workings of the Query Optimizer. Examples of goal oriented hints include the OPTIMIZER FOR or FAST N hints. Almost all the remaining hints covered in this chapter are physical hints.

Locking hints do not affect plan selection, so they will not be covered here. Plan guides, which allow you to apply a hint to a query without changing the code in your application, and the USE PLAN query hint, which allows you to force the Query Optimizer to use a specified execution plan for a query, are covered separately, later in the chapter.

In the next few sections, I will discuss hints affecting joins, join order, aggregations, index scans or seeks, views, and so on. Note that, with a very simple database like `AdventureWorks`, the Query Optimizer will most likely give you an optimal plan for all of the examples in this chapter, so I am just looking for alternate plans for demonstration purposes.

Joins

We can explicitly ask the Query Optimizer to use any of the available join algorithms: Nested Loops, Merge and Hash Join. We could do this at the query level, in which case all the existing joins in the query will be affected, or we can specify it at the join level, impacting only that join. However, this last choice will also impact the join order, as will be explained in the **FORCE ORDER** section.

Let's focus on join hints at the query level first; in this case, the join algorithm is specified using the **OPTION** clause. You can also specify two of the three available joins, which basically asks the Query Optimizer to exclude the third physical join operator from consideration. The decision between which of the remaining two joins to use will be cost-based. For example, the following unhinted query will produce the plan in Figure 7-1, which uses a Hash Join.

```
SELECT FirstName, LastName
FROM Person.Contact AS C
    JOIN Sales.Individual AS I
        ON C.ContactID = I.ContactID
```

Listing 7-1.

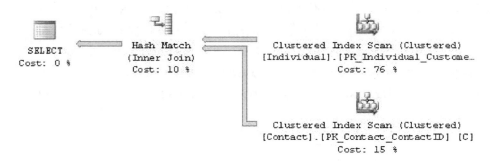

Figure 7-1:   Execution plan using a Hash Join.

On the other hand, the following query will request the Query Optimizer to exclude a Hash Join by requesting either a Nested Loops or Merge Join. In this case, the Query Optimizer chooses a Merge Join, as shown in the plan in Figure 7-2.

```
SELECT FirstName, LastName
FROM Person.Contact AS C
    JOIN Sales.Individual AS I
        ON C.ContactID = I.ContactID
OPTION (LOOP JOIN, MERGE JOIN)
```

Listing 7-2.

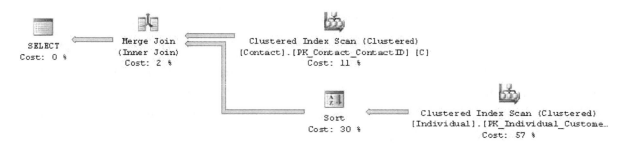

Figure 7-2:   Execution plan excluding a Hash Join.

Join hints can not only force the joins we explicitly specify in our query text, but can also impact most of the joins introduced by the Query Optimizer, such as foreign key validation or cascading actions. Other joins, like the Nested Loops used in a bookmark lookup, cannot be changed, as it would defeat the purpose of using the bookmark lookup in the first place. For example, in the following query, the hint to use a Merge Join will be ignored, as shown in the plan in Figure 7-3.

```
SELECT AddressID, City, StateProvinceID, ModifiedDate FROM Person.Address
WHERE City = 'Santa Fe'
OPTION (MERGE JOIN)
```

Listing 7-3.

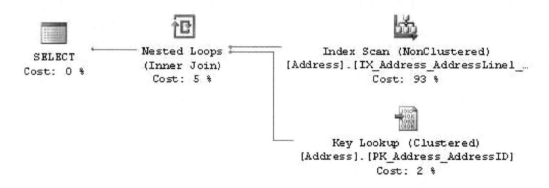

Figure 7-3:   Hint ignored in a bookmark lookup example.

As mentioned earlier, hints cannot force the Query Optimizer to generate invalid plans, so the query in Listing 7-4 will not compile, as both Merge and Hash Joins require an equality operator on the join predicate. Trying to execute this query will return the error message shown in Listing 7-5.

```
SELECT FirstName, LastName
FROM Person.Contact AS C
    JOIN Sales.Individual AS I
        ON C.ContactID > I.ContactID
WHERE C.ContactID > 19974
OPTION (MERGE JOIN)
```

Listing 7-4.

```
Msg 8622, Level 16, State 1, Line 2
Query processor could not produce a query plan because of the hints defined in this query.
Resubmit the query without specifying any hints and without using SET FORCEPLAN.
```

Listing 7-5.

However, as mentioned before, keep in mind that using the query-level hint will impact the entire query. If you need explicit control over *each* join in a query, then you can use ANSI-style join hints, the benefit of which is that a join type can be individually selected for every join in the plan. However, be warned that using ANSI join hints will also add the behavior of the FORCE ORDER hint, which asks to preserve the join *order* and aggregation placement, as indicated by the query syntax. This behavior will be explained in the FORCE ORDER section, later in this chapter.

In the meantime, let me show you an example. The following query without hints will produce the execution plan shown in Figure 7-4:

```
SELECT FirstName, LastName
FROM Person.Contact AS C
    JOIN Sales.Individual AS I
        ON C.ContactID = I.ContactID
    JOIN Sales.Customer AS Cu
        ON I.CustomerID = Cu.CustomerID
WHERE Cu.CustomerType = 'I'
```

Listing 7-6.

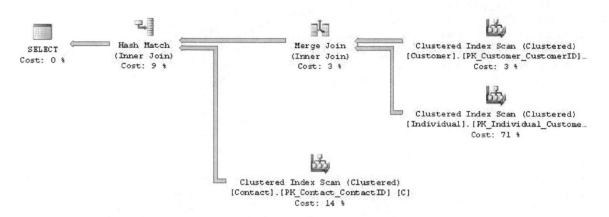

Figure 7-4: Execution plan without hints.

The next query explicitly requests a Hash Join and a Nested Loops Join, and will produce a different plan, as shown in Figure 7-5. Notice that the **INNER** keyword is required this time.

```
SELECT FirstName, LastName
FROM Person.Contact AS C
    INNER HASH JOIN Sales.Individual AS I
        ON C.ContactID = I.ContactID
    INNER LOOP JOIN Sales.Customer AS Cu
        ON I.CustomerID = Cu.CustomerID
WHERE Cu.CustomerType = 'I'
```

Listing 7-7.

In addition, the related warning (Listing 7-8) is shown in the Messages tab when the code is executed using Management Studio.

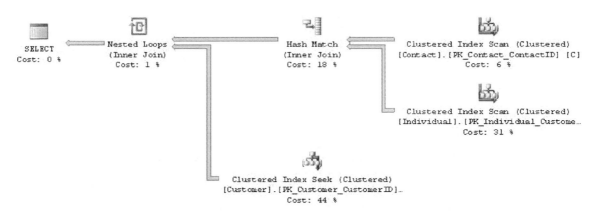

Figure 7-5: Execution plan with ANSI-style join hints.

```
Warning: The join order has been enforced because a local join hint is used.
```

Listing 7-8.

This warning indicates that not only was the join algorithm forced, but the join order was forced as well, that is, the tables were joined using exactly the order specified in the query text.

Aggregations

Just like join algorithms, aggregation algorithms can also be forced by using the GROUP hints. Specifically, the ORDER GROUP hint requests that the Query Optimizer uses a Stream Aggregate algorithm and the HASH GROUP hint requests a Hash Aggregate algorithm. These hints can be specified only at the query level, so they will impact all of the aggregation operations in the query. To see the effects of this, take a look at the unhinted query in Listing 7-9, which produces the plan on Figure 7-6 using a Stream Aggregate.

```
SELECT SalesOrderID, COUNT(*)
FROM Sales.SalesOrderDetail
GROUP BY SalesOrderID
```

Listing 7-9.

Figure 7-6:   Execution plan using a Stream Aggregate.

Since the `SalesOrderDetail` table has a clustered index on the `SalesOrderID` column, and so the data is already sorted on the **GROUP BY** column, using a Stream Aggregate operator is the obvious choice. However, the following query will force a Hash Aggregate operator, and will produce the plan shown in Figure 7-7, which will, of course, make the query more expensive than necessary.

```
SELECT SalesOrderID, COUNT(*)
FROM Sales.SalesOrderDetail
GROUP BY SalesOrderID
OPTION (HASH GROUP)
```

Listing 7-10.

Figure 7-7:   Execution plan with a HASH GROUP hint.

On the other hand, a scalar aggregation will always use a Stream Aggregate operator. Trying to force a Hash Aggregate on a scalar aggregation, as in the following query, will trigger the compilation error shown in Listing 7-5, complaining about the hints defined in the query.

```
SELECT COUNT(*)
FROM Sales.SalesOrderDetail
OPTION (HASH GROUP)
```

Listing 7-11.

FORCE ORDER

The **FORCE ORDER** hint can give the user full control over the join and aggregation placement in an execution plan. Specifically, the **FORCE ORDER** hint asks the Query Optimizer to preserve the join order and aggregation placement as indicated by the query syntax. Notice, also, that the **ANSI**-style join hints explained before can also give you control of the join order, in addition to control over the choice of the join algorithm. Both the **FORCE ORDER** and **ANSI**-style join hints are very powerful, and because of that they need to be used with caution. As explained earlier in this book, finding an optimum join order is a critical part of the query optimization process, and also a challenging one, because the sheer number of possible join orders can be huge even with queries involving only a few tables. What this boils down to is that, by using the **FORCE ORDER** hint, you are attempting to optimize the join order yourself.

You can use the **FORCE ORDER** hint to obtain any form of query, like left-deep trees, bushy trees or right-deep trees, explained in *Chapter 1, Introduction to Query Optimization*. The Query Optimizer will usually produce a left-deep tree plan, but you can force bushy trees or right-deep trees by doing things like changing the location of the **ON** clause on the join predicate, using subqueries, parenthesis, etc. Be aware that forcing join order does not affect the simplification phase of query optimization, and some joins may still be removed if needed, as explained in *Chapter 5, The Optimization Process*.

If you do need to change the join order of a query for some reason, you can try starting with the join order recommended by the Query Optimizer, and change only the part which you think is suffering from a problem, such as cardinality estimation errors. You can also follow the practices that the Query Optimizer itself would follow, as explained in *Chapter 2, The Execution Engine*. For example, if you are forcing a Hash Join, select the smallest table as the build input, or if you're forcing a Nested Loops Join, use small tables in the outer input and the tables with indexes as the inner input. You could also start by joining small tables first, or tables that can help to filter out the most possible number of rows.

Let me show you an example. The query in Listing 7-12, without hints, will show you the plan on Figure 7-8.

```
SELECT FirstName, LastName
FROM Person.Contact AS C
    JOIN Sales.Individual AS I
        ON C.ContactID = I.ContactID
    JOIN Sales.Customer AS Cu
        ON I.CustomerID = Cu.CustomerID
WHERE Cu.CustomerType = 'I'
```

Listing 7-12.

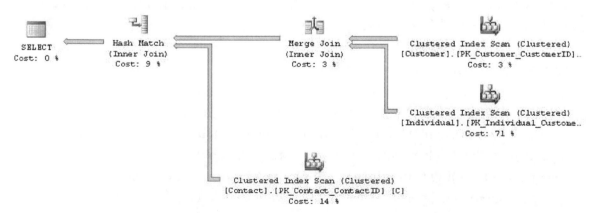

Figure 7-8:   Execution plan without hints.

As you can see, the Query Optimizer does not follow the join order you have specified in the query syntax; instead it found a better join order based on cost decisions. Now let's see what happens if we change the query to use non-ANSI joins, by removing the ON clauses and separating the table names with commas, and finally adding a FORCE ORDER hint to the query. It will produce the plan in Figure 7-9.

```
SELECT FirstName, LastName
FROM Person.Contact AS C, Sales.Individual AS I, Sales.Customer AS Cu
WHERE I.CustomerID = Cu.CustomerID
AND C.ContactID = I.ContactID
AND Cu.CustomerType = 'I'
OPTION (FORCE ORDER)
```

Listing 7-13.

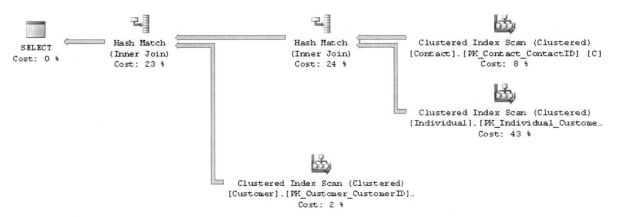

Figure 7-9:   Execution plan with FORCE ORDER hint.

In this query using non-ANSI joins and the FORCE ORDER hint, the tables will be joined in the order specified in the query, and by default will create a left-deep tree. On the other hand, if you are using the FORCE ORDER hint in a query *with* ANSI joins, SQL Server will consider the location of the ON clauses to define the location of the joins. As an example of this phenomenon, the query in Listing 7-14 will create a similar plan to the one shown in Figure 7-9 but, in this case, SQL Server *is* considering the location of the ON clauses and, as requested by the clause `ON C.ContactID = I.ContactID`, it's joining the `Contact` and `Individual` tables first.

```
SELECT FirstName, LastName
FROM Person.Contact AS C
    JOIN Sales.Individual AS I
        ON C.ContactID = I.ContactID
    JOIN Sales.Customer AS Cu
        ON I.CustomerID = Cu.CustomerID
WHERE Cu.CustomerType = 'I'
OPTION (FORCE ORDER)
```
Listing 7-14.

In the next query, we are creating a right-deep tree (just to demonstrate that it's possible), as we are requesting to join the `Individual` and `Customer` tables first, as requested by the `ON I.CustomerID = Cu.CustomerID` clause. The resulting execution plan is shown on Figure 7-10.

```
SELECT FirstName, LastName
FROM Person.Contact AS C
    JOIN Sales.Individual AS I
    JOIN Sales.Customer AS Cu
        ON I.CustomerID = Cu.CustomerID
        ON C.ContactID = I.ContactID
WHERE Cu.CustomerType = 'I'
OPTION (FORCE ORDER)
```
Listing 7-15.

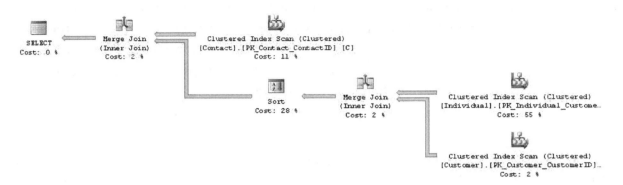

Figure 7-10: Plan forcing a right-deep tree.

In addition to taking control of join orders, as mentioned in the introduction of this section, **FORCE ORDER** can also be used to force the order of aggregations. Consider this unhinted example, which produces the plan seen in Figure 7-11:

```
SELECT c.CustomerID, COUNT(*)
FROM Sales.Customer c JOIN Sales.SalesOrderHeader o
ON c.CustomerID = o.CustomerID
GROUP BY c.CustomerID
```

Listing 7-16.

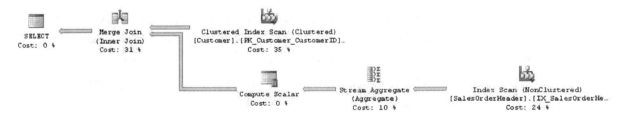

Figure 7-11: Plan with aggregation before the join.

As you can see, in this case the Query Optimizer decided to perform the aggregation before the join. (Remember that, as mentioned in *Chapter 2, The Execution Engine*, the Query Optimizer can decide to perform aggregations before or after a join, depending on the cost.) By adding a **FORCE ORDER** hint, as in the following query, the aggregation will be moved to after the join, as shown in Figure 7-12.

```
SELECT c.CustomerID, COUNT(*)
FROM Sales.Customer c JOIN Sales.SalesOrderHeader o
ON c.CustomerID = o.CustomerID
GROUP BY c.CustomerID
OPTION (FORCE ORDER)
```

Listing 7-17.

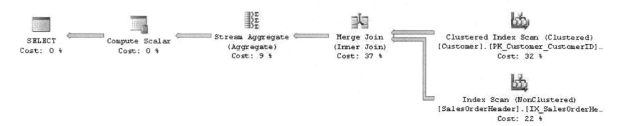

Figure 7-12: Plan with aggregation after the join.

Finally, a related statement, **SET FORCEPLAN**, can also be used to preserve the join order, as indicated in the **FROM** clause of a query, but it will request Nested Loops Joins only. A difference between that and the hints shown so far is that this statement needs to be turned on, and will stay in effect until turned off. For more information regarding the **SET FORCEPLAN** statement, please refer to Books Online.

INDEX and FORCESEEK hints

The INDEX and FORCESEEK hints are table hints, and we'll consider each in turn. The INDEX hint can be used to request the Query Optimizer to use a specific index or indexes. Either the index id or the name of the index can be used as a target for the Query Optimizer, but a name is the recommended way, as we do not have control of the index id values for non-clustered indexes. However, if you still want to use index id values, or you are interested in them for some other reason, they can be found on the index_id column on sys.indexes; index id 0 is a heap, index id 1 is a clustered index, and a value greater than 1 is a non-clustered index. On a query using a heap, using the INDEX(0) hint results in a Table Scan operator being used, and INDEX(1) returns an error message. However, a query with a clustered index can use both values: INDEX(0) will force a Clustered Index Scan, and INDEX(1) can use either a Clustered Index Scan or a Clustered Index Seek. On the other hand, the FORCESEEK hint can be used to force the Query Optimizer to use an Index Seek operation, and can work on both clustered or non-clustered indexes. It can also work in combination with the INDEX hint, as we'll see later.

In addition to helping to improve the performance of your queries, in some cases you may also want to consider using an index hint to minimize lock contention or deadlocks. Notice that, when you use an INDEX hint, your query becomes dependent on the existence of the specified index, and it will not compile (or will stop working) if that index is removed. Using FORCESEEK without an available index will also result in an error, as shown later in this section.

You can also use the INDEX hint to avoid a bookmark lookup operation, as in the example shown in Listing 7-18. Since the Query Optimizer estimates that only a few records will be returned by the next query, it decides to use an Index Seek – Key Lookup combination, as shown on Figure 7-13.

```
SELECT * FROM Sales.SalesOrderDetail
WHERE ProductID = 897
```

Listing 7-18.

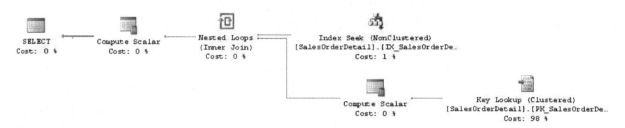

Figure 7-13: Plan without hints.

However, suppose that you want to avoid a bookmark lookup operation; you can use the **INDEX** table hint to force a table scan instead (which could be the scan of either a heap or a clustered index). The following query will force the use of a Clustered Index Scan operator, as shown on the plan on Figure 7-14.

```
SELECT * FROM Sales.SalesOrderDetail
WITH (INDEX(0))
WHERE ProductID = 897
```

Listing 7-19.

Figure 7-14: Plan with an **INDEX** hint.

Using **INDEX(1)** in this example would give a similar result, as SQL Server cannot use the clustered index to do an Index Seek operation; the clustered key is on **SalesOrderID** and **SalesOrderDetailID**, so the only viable choice is to scan the clustered index.

Of course, you can also force the opposite operation. In the following example, the Query Optimizer estimates that a high number of records will be returned, and so it decides to use a Clustered Index Scan, similar to the plan previously shown in Figure 7-14.

```
SELECT * FROM Sales.SalesOrderDetail
WHERE ProductID = 870
```
Listing 7-20.

Since we have an available index on ProductID (IX_SalesOrderDetail_ProductID), we can force the plan to use that index.

```
SELECT * FROM Sales.SalesOrderDetail
WITH (INDEX(IX_SalesOrderDetail_ProductID))
WHERE ProductID = 870
```
Listing 7-21.

This query will produce a new plan, similar to the one in Figure 7-13 which, in fact, is using an Index Seek on the IX_SalesOrderDetail_ProductID index, and a Key Lookup to the base table, which in this case is the clustered index.

You can also achieve a similar result by forcing a seek using the FORCESEEK table hint, which is new in SQL Server 2008. The following query will create a plan similar to the one shown previously in Figure 7-13.

```
SELECT * FROM Sales.SalesOrderDetail
WITH (FORCESEEK)
WHERE ProductID = 870
```
Listing 7-22.

You can even combine both hints to obtain the same results, as in the next query.

```
SELECT * FROM Sales.SalesOrderDetail
WITH (INDEX(IX_SalesOrderDetail_ProductID), FORCESEEK)
WHERE ProductID = 870
```

Listing 7-23.

Using **FORCESEEK** when SQL Server cannot do an Index Seek operation, as in the following query, will not compile, and will instead return an error message.

```
SELECT * FROM Sales.SalesOrderDetail
WITH (FORCESEEK)
WHERE OrderQty = 1
```

Listing 7-24.

FAST N

FAST N is one of the so-called goal oriented hints, as it does not indicate what physical operators to use, but instead just specifies what goal the plan is trying to achieve. This hint is used to optimize a query to retrieve the first N rows of results as quickly as possible. It can help in situations where only the first few rows returned by a query are relevant, and perhaps you won't be using the remaining records of the query at all. The price to pay for achieving this speed is that retrieving those remaining records may take longer than if you had used a plan without this hint. In other words, since the query is optimized to retrieve the first N records as soon as possible, retrieving all the records returned by the query may be very expensive.

The Query Optimizer usually accomplishes this FAST N goal by avoiding any blocking operators, like Sort, Hash Join or Hash Aggregation, so the client submitting the query does not have to wait before the first records are produced. Let's see an example; run the following query, which returns the plan shown in Figure 7-15.

```
SELECT * FROM Sales.SalesOrderDetail
ORDER BY ProductID
```

Listing 7-25.

Figure 7-15:   Plan without a hint.

In this case, the Sort operator is the most effective way to get the records sorted by ProductID if you want to see the entire query output. However, since Sort is a blocking operator, SQL Server will not produce any record until the sort is completed. Now, supposing that your application wants to see a page with 20 records at a time, you can use the FAST hint to get these 20 records as quickly as possible, as seen in the next query.

```
SELECT * FROM Sales.SalesOrderDetail
ORDER BY ProductID
OPTION (FAST 20)
```

Listing 7-26.

This time, the new plan, seen in Figure 7-16, scans an available non-clustered index while performing Key Lookups to the clustered table. Since this plan uses random I/Os, it would be very expensive for the entire query, but it will achieve the goal of returning the first 20 records very quickly.

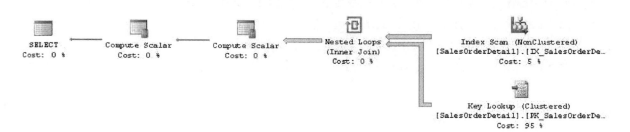

Figure 7-16: Plan using a FAST N hint.

There is also a **FASTFIRSTROW** hint, but it is not as flexible as **FAST N** , as you can specify any number for N. Essentially, **FASTFIRSTROW** would be the same as specifying the **FAST 1** hint.

NOEXPAND, EXPAND VIEWS hints

Before talking about the **NOEXPAND** and **EXPAND VIEWS** hints, let me explain the default behavior of queries when using indexed views so that you can see how these hints can change this behavior.

As explained in *Chapter 5, The Optimization Process*, SQL Server expands views in the early steps of query optimization during binding, when a view reference is expanded to include the view definition; for example, to directly include the tables used in the view. This behavior is the same for every edition of SQL Server. Later on in the optimization process, but only in the Enterprise edition, SQL Server may match the query to an existing indexed view. So, basically, the view was expanded at the beginning but was later matched to an existing indexed view. The **EXPAND VIEWS** hint removes the matching step, thus making sure the views are expanded but not matched at the end of the optimization process. So this hint only has an effect in SQL Server Enterprise edition.

On the other hand, the **NOEXPAND** hint asks SQL Server not to expand any views at all, and to try to use any existing indexed view instead. This hint works in every SQL Server edition, and it is the only way (when using a SQL Server edition other than Enterprise) to ask SQL Server to match an existing view.

Here's an example. Create an indexed view on **AdventureWorks** by running the following code:

```
CREATE VIEW v_test WITH SCHEMABINDING AS
SELECT SalesOrderID, COUNT_BIG(*) as cnt
FROM Sales.SalesOrderDetail
GROUP BY SalesOrderID
GO
CREATE UNIQUE CLUSTERED INDEX ix_test ON v_test(SalesOrderID);
```

Listing 7-27.

Next, run the following query:

```
SELECT SalesOrderID, COUNT(*)
FROM Sales.SalesOrderDetail
GROUP BY SalesOrderID
```

Listing 7-28.

If you are using SQL Server Enterprise edition (or the Enterprise Evaluation or Developer editions, which share the same database engine edition), you will get the following plan, which actually matches the existing indexed view, as shown in the plan in Figure 7-17.

Figure 7-17: Plan using an existing indexed view.

Alternatively, you can use the **EXPAND VIEWS** hint, as in the following query, to avoid matching the index view. You will get the plan seen in Figure 7-18.

```
SELECT SalesOrderID, COUNT(*)
FROM Sales.SalesOrderDetail
GROUP BY SalesOrderID
OPTION (EXPAND VIEWS)
```

Listing 7-29.

Figure 7-18: Plan using the **EXPAND VIEWS** hint.

Finally, drop the indexed view you just have created:

```
DROP VIEW v_test
```

Listing 7-30.

Plan Guides

There might be situations when you need to apply a hint to a query, but you are unable or unwilling to change your query code or your application. As mentioned earlier, a common situation where this occurs is if you are working with third-party code or applications, which you cannot change.

Plan guides, a new feature introduced with SQL Server 2005, can help you in these instances. Plan guides essentially work by keeping a list of queries on the server, along with the hints you want to apply to them. To use a plan guide, you need to provide SQL Server with the query that you want to optimize, and either a query hint using the `OPTION` clause, or an XML plan using the `USE PLAN` hint, which will be explained in the next section. When the query is optimized, SQL Server will apply the hint requested in the plan guide definition. You can also specify NULL as a hint in your plan guide to remove an existing hint in your application.

As well as allowing you to apply hints to code which you can't or don't want to change, plan guides make it easier to apply, update, and remove query hints. Plan guides can also match queries in different contexts; for example, a stored procedure, a user-defined scalar function, or a stand-alone statement which is not part of any database object.

You can use the `sp_create_plan_guide` stored procedure to create a plan guide, and the `sp_control_plan_guide` to drop, enable or disable plan guides. For more details on how to use these stored procedures, you should investigate Books Online, which has much more detail than we could cover here. You can see which plan guides are defined in your database by looking at the `sys.plan_guides` catalog view.

To make sure that the query in the plan guide definition matches the query being executed, especially for stand-alone statements, you can use the Profiler's `Plan Guide Successful` event class, which will show whether an execution plan was successfully created using a plan guide. On the other hand, the `Plan Guide Unsuccessful` event will show if SQL Server was unable to create an execution plan using a plan guide, meaning that the query was instead optimized without it. You can see the `Plan Guide Unsuccessful` event, for example, when trying to force a Merge or Hash Join with a non-equality operator in the join condition, as shown in Listing 7-4, earlier in this chapter.

Let's see an example of these events. Suppose we want to use plan guides to avoid a Merge or Hash Join in our previous query, in order to avoid high memory usage. Before running this code, open a SQL Server Profiler session, connect it to your instance of SQL Server, select the blank template to start a new trace definition, and select both `Plan Guide Successful` and `Plan Guide Unsuccessful` on the **Performance** section of the **Events** tab, and then start the trace.

Next, create the following stored procedure:

```
CREATE PROCEDURE test
AS
SELECT FirstName, LastName
FROM Person.Contact AS C JOIN Sales.Individual AS I
ON C.ContactID = I.ContactID
```

Listing 7-31.

Before creating a plan guide, execute the stored procedure and display its execution plan to verify that it is using a Hash Join operator.

```
EXEC test
```

Listing 7-32.

Once you've confirmed that, create a plan guide to force the query to use a Nested Loops Join.

```
EXEC sp_create_plan_guide
    @name = N'plan_guide_test',
    @stmt = N'SELECT FirstName, LastName
    FROM Person.Contact AS C JOIN Sales.Individual AS I
    ON C.ContactID = I.ContactID',
    @type = N'OBJECT',
    @module_or_batch = N'test',
    @params = NULL,
    @hints = N'OPTION (LOOP JOIN)';
```

Listing 7-33.

Now, if you execute the stored procedure again, you can verify that it is now using a Nested Loops Join operator, as shown in the plan in Figure 7-19.

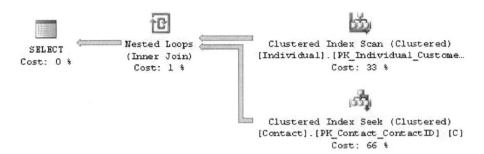

Figure 7-19: Plan using a plan guide.

In addition, during this execution SQL Server Profiler should capture a **Plan Guide Successful** event, showing that SQL Server was able to use the defined plan guide. The **TextData** column will show the name of the plan guide, which in this case is **plan_guide_test**, as shown in Figure 7-20.

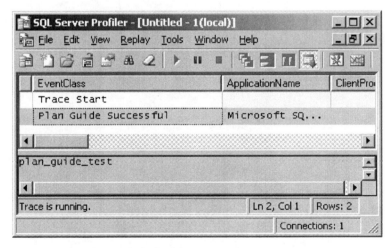

Figure 7-20: Capturing a **Plan Guide Successful** event.

Once you've created your plan guide, you can enable or disable it at any time. For example, the following statement will disable the previous plan guide, and the stored procedure will again use a Hash Join when executed.

```
EXEC sp_control_plan_guide N'DISABLE', N'plan_guide_test';
```

Listing 7-34.

To enable the plan guide again, use:

```
EXEC sp_control_plan_guide N'ENABLE', N'plan_guide_test';
```

Listing 7-35.

Finally, to clean up, drop both the plan guide and the stored procedure. Note that you need to drop the plan guide first, as you cannot drop a stored procedure that it is currently referenced by a plan guide.

```
EXEC sp_control_plan_guide N'DROP', N'plan_guide_test';
DROP PROCEDURE test
```

Listing 7-36.

USE PLAN

Finally, let's take a look at the USE PLAN query hint, which was introduced with SQL Server 2005. This takes the use of hints to the extreme by allowing the user to specify an entire execution plan as a target to be used to optimize a query. The USE PLAN hint is useful when you know that a better plan than the Query Optimizer's suggestion exists.

This can be the case, for example, when a better performing plan was produced in the past, or in a different system, or even in a previous version of SQL Server.

The plan should be specified in XML format, and you will usually use SQL Server itself to generate the XML text for the desired plan, as it can be extremely difficult to write an XML plan manually.

The USE PLAN hint can force most of the specified plan properties, including the tree structure, join order, join algorithms, aggregations, sorting and unions, and index operations like scans, seeks and intersections, so that only the transformation rules that can be useful in finding the desired plan are executed. In addition, USE PLAN now supports UPDATE statements (INSERT, UPDATE, DELETE and MERGE), which was not the case when the hint was first introduced in SQL Server 2005. Some statements still not supported include full-text or distributed queries, and queries with dynamic, keyset-driven and forward-only cursors.

Suppose we have the same query we saw in the plan guides section, which produces a Hash Join ...

```
SELECT FirstName, LastName
FROM Person.Contact AS C JOIN Sales.Individual AS I
ON C.ContactID = I.ContactID
```

Listing 7-37.

... and suppose that you want SQL Server to use a different execution plan, which we can generate using a hint:

```
SELECT FirstName, LastName
FROM Person.Contact AS C JOIN Sales.Individual AS I
ON C.ContactID = I.ContactID
OPTION (LOOP JOIN)
```

Listing 7-38.

You can force this new plan to use a Nested Loops Join instead of a Hash Join. In order to accomplish that, display the new XML plan (by right-clicking on the graphical plan and selecting **Show Execution Plan XML ...**), copy it to an editor, replace all of the single quotes with double quotes, and then copy the plan to the query, as shown below.

```
SELECT FirstName, LastName
FROM Person.Contact AS C JOIN Sales.Individual AS I
ON C.ContactID = I.ContactID
OPTION (USE PLAN N'<?xml version="1.0" encoding="utf-16"?> …
</ShowPlanXML>')
```
Listing 7-39.

Of course, the XML plan is too long to display here, so I've just displayed the start and end. Make sure the query ends with **')** after the XML plan. Running the **SELECT** statement above will request SQL Server to try to use the indicated plan, and the query will be executed with a Nested Loops Join, as requested in the provided XML execution plan.

You can combine both plan guides and the **USE PLAN** query hint to force a specific execution plan in a situation where you don't want to change the text of the original query. The following (and final) query will use the same example included in Listing 7-33 in the plan guides section, together with the XML plan generated a moment ago. Note the use of two single quotes before the XML plan specification, meaning that, this time, the query text needs to end with **'')'**.

```
EXEC sp_create_plan_guide
    @name = N'plan_guide_test',
@stmt = N'SELECT FirstName, LastName
    FROM Person.Contact AS C JOIN Sales.Individual AS I
    ON C.ContactID = I.ContactID',
    @type = N'OBJECT',
    @module_or_batch = N'test',
    @params = NULL,
    @hints = N'OPTION (USE PLAN N''<?xml version="1.0" encoding="utf-16"?> …
```
Listing 7-40.

Finally, bear in mind that, when the USE PLAN hint is used directly in a query, an invalid plan will make the query fail. However, when the USE PLAN hint is used in a plan guide, an invalid plan will simply compile the query without the requested hint, as mentioned in the previous section.

Summary

The Query Optimizer typically selects a good execution plan for your queries, but there may still be cases when you are not getting good performance from a selected plan, even after extensive troubleshooting. Although hints can be used to improve the performance of a query in these cases by directly taking control of the execution plan selection, they should always be used with caution, and only as a last resort. You should also be aware that code using hints will require additional maintenance, and is significantly less flexible to changes in your database, application or software upgrades.

This chapter explained how to use hints to force join algorithms, join order, aggregations, indexes for both scan or seek operations, and the use of indexed views, among other behaviors. We also examined the use of plan guides to implement hints without changing the code of your (or third-party) applications, and the ability of the USE PLAN hint to specify an entire XML plan as the target of the optimization.

Finally, my hope is that the chapters of this book have provided you with the knowledge needed to write better queries, and to give the Query Optimizer the information it needs to produce efficient execution plans. At the same time, I hope you've seen more about how to get the information you need to diagnose and troubleshoot the cases when (despite your best efforts) you are *not* getting a good plan. In addition, having seen how the Query Optimizer works, and some of the limitations this complex piece of software still faces today, you can be better prepared to decide when and how hints can be used to improve the performance of your queries.

Index

SQL Server
and .NET tools
from Red Gate Software

redgate®

ingeniously simple tools

SQL Compare® $595

Compare and synchronize SQL Server database schemas

- ↗ Eliminate mistakes migrating database changes from dev, to test, to production
- ↗ Speed up the deployment of new databse schema updates
- ↗ Find and fix errors caused by differences between databases
- ↗ Compare and synchronize within SSMS

> **"I bless the day we bought SQL Compare – it saves me time so often. Must have paid for itself a hundred times over"**
> **Bill Geake** Martin Currie Investment Management

SQL Data Compare™ $595

Compares and synchronizes SQL Server database contents

- ↗ Save time by automatically comparing and synchronizing your data
- ↗ Copy lookup data from development databases to staging or production
- ↗ Quickly fix problems by restoring damaged or missing data to a single row
- ↗ Compare and synchronize data within SSMS

> **"We use SQL Data Compare daily and it has become an indispensable part of delivering our service to our customers. It has also streamlined our daily update process and cut back literally a good solid hour per day."**
> **George Pantela** GPAnalysis.com

SQL Prompt™ $295
Write, edit, and explore SQL effortlessly

- ↗ Write SQL smoothly, with code-completion and SQL snippets
- ↗ Reformat SQL to a preferred style
- ↗ Keep databases tidy by finding invalid objects automatically
- ↗ Save time and effort with script summaries, smart object renaming and more

> **"SQL Prompt is hands-down one of the coolest applications I've used. Makes querying/developing so much easier and faster."**
> **Jorge Segarra** University Community Hospital

SQL Source Control $295
Connect your existing source control system to SQL Server

- ↗ Bring all the benefits of source control to your database
- ↗ Work directly in SQL Server Management Studio, not with offline scripts
- ↗ Connect your database to Team Foundation Server (TFS), Subversion (SVN), Vault or VSS
- ↗ Track changes so you know who changed what, when, and why
- ↗ Help teams stay in sync by easily getting the latest database version

> **"After using SQL Source Control for several months, I wondered how I got by before. Highly recommended, it has paid for itself several times over"**
> **Ben Ashley** Fast Floor

Visit **www.red-gate.com** for a 28-day, free trial

SQL Monitor™

Proactive SQL Server performance monitoring and alerting

↗ Intuitive overviews at global, machine, SQL Server and database levels for up-to-the minute performance data

↗ SQL Monitor's web UI means you can check your server health and performance on the go with many mobile devices, including tablets

↗ Intelligent SQL Server alerts via email and an alert inbox in the UI, so you know about problems first

↗ Comprehensive historical data, so you can go back in time to identify the source of a problem, fast

↗ Generate reports via the UI and with SQL Server Reporting Services

↗ Investigate long-running queries, SQL deadlocks, blocked processes, and more, to resolve problems sooner

↗ Fast, simple installation and administration

> **"Being web based, SQL Monitor is readily available to you, wherever you may be on your network. You can check on your servers from almost any location, via most mobile devices that support a web browser."**
>
> **Jonathan Allen** Senior DBA, Careers South West Ltd

SQL Virtual Restore™ $495

Rapidly mount live, fully functional databases direct from backups

↗ Turn backups into live databases for quick and easy access to data, without requiring a physical restore

↗ Databases mounted with SQL Virtual Restore are live and fully functional, just like a regular database

↗ Mounting a backup as a live database requires less storage space than a regular physical restore

↗ Perform smart object level recovery - SQL Virtual Restore is ACID compliant and gives you access to full, transactionally consistent data, with all objects visible and available

↗ Verify your backups - run DBCC CHECKDB against databases mounted by SQL Virtual Restore, without requiring the space and time for a full restore

> **"SQL Virtual Restore offers several important benefits to DBAs that a standard restore can't provide: substantial space savings, and substantial restore time savings."**
> **Brad McGehee** Director of DBA Education, Red Gate Software

HYPERBAC® POWERED

SQL Storage Compress™ $1,595

Silent data compression to optimize SQL Server storage

↗ Reduce the storage footprint of live SQL Server databases by up to 90% to save on space and hardware costs

↗ Works seamlessly with compressed files – databases compressed with SQL Storage Compress are live and fully functional

↗ Integrates seamlessly with SQL Server and does not require any configuration changes

↗ Protect the data in your live databases with 256-bit AES encryption

> **"SQL Storage Compress is very easy to use and self-maintained. Everything is done at the OS level, which makes it very easy to implement."**
> **Qian Ye** Senior Database Administrator, National Institute of Health

HYPERBAC® POWERED

Visit **www.red-gate.com** for a 14-day, free trial

SQL Toolbelt™ $1,995

The essential SQL Server tools for
database professionals

You can buy our acclaimed SQL Server tools individually or bundled. Our most popular deal is
the SQL Toolbelt: fourteen of our SQL Server tools in a single installer, with **a combined value of
$5,930 but an actual price of $1,995**, a saving of 66%.

Fully compatible with SQL Server 2000, 2005, and 2008.

SQL Toolbelt contains:

- ↗ **SQL Compare Pro**
- ↗ **SQL Data Compare Pro**
- ↗ **SQL Source Control**
- ↗ **SQL Backup Pro**
- ↗ **SQL Response**
- ↗ **SQL Prompt Pro**
- ↗ **SQL Data Generator**

- ↗ **SQL Doc**
- ↗ **SQL Dependency Tracker**
- ↗ **SQL Packager**
- ↗ **SQL Multi Script Unlimited**
- ↗ **SQL Refactor**
- ↗ **SQL Comparison SDK**
- ↗ **SQL Object Level Recovery Native**

> **"The SQL Toolbelt provides tools
> that database developers, as well
> as DBAs, should not live without."**
>
> **William Van Orden** Senior Database Developer,
> Lockheed Martin

Performance Tuning with SQL Server Dynamic Management Views

Louis Davidson and Tim Ford

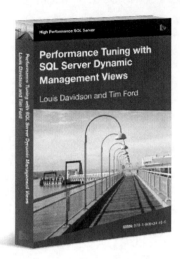

This is the book that will de-mystify the process of using Dynamic Management Views to collect the information you need to troubleshoot SQL Server problems. It will highlight the core techniques and "patterns" that you need to master, and will provide a core set of scripts that you can use and adapt for your own requirements.

ISBN: 978-1-906434-47-2
Published: October 2010

Defensive Database Programming

Alex Kuznetsov

Inside this book, you will find dozens of practical, defensive programming techniques that will improve the quality of your T-SQL code and increase its resilience and robustness.

ISBN: 978-1-906434-49-6
Published: June 2010

SQL Server Hardware

Glenn Berry

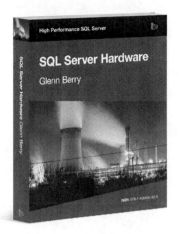

SQL Server Hardware will provide the fundamental knowledge and resources you need to make intelligent decisions about choice, and optimal installation and configuration, of SQL Server hardware, operating system and the SQL Server RDBMS

ISBN: 978-1-906434-63-2
Published: Coming Soon

The Red Gate Guide to SQL Server Team-based Development

Phil Factor, Grant Fritchey, Alex Kuznetsov, and Mladen Prajdić

This book shows how to use of mixture of home-grown scripts, native SQL Server tools, and tools from the Red Gate SQL Toolbelt, to successfully develop database applications in a team environment, and make database development as similar as possible to "normal" development.

ISBN: 978-1-906434-59-5
Published: November 2010

CPSIA information can be obtained at www.ICGtesting.com
Printed in the USA
LVOW030006090512

280883LV00015B/51/P